THE
INVISIBLE
BLACK NURSE

NAVIGATING RACE-isms
A GUIDE ON BECOMING VISIB_E: LOVE COVERS ALL`

ORA ROBINSON, Ph.D., RN.

Published by AMJ Productions & Publications.

Cover design by University of Moguls Publishing and Design www.universityofmoguls.com
Interior Design by Empowered Design Studios
www.facebook.com/EmpoweredDesignStudio

ISBN - 979-8-9892328-2-6

For speaking engagements and bulk book orders:

Ora V. Robinson
nurseora@outlook.com

Website:
www.TheinvisibleBlacknurse.com

Instagram: @nurseora_

Twitter: @nurseora

Facebook:
www.facebook.com/nurseora

DEDICATION

Primarily, to the almighty God, my Lord Jesus Christ. My parents, Mae C. King, and David Lee King (deceased) encouraged me to move out of my comfort zone and share my gifts with the world. To my sisters Vanessa E. King and Rosaland A. King (deceased) who offered continued encouragement to write the book even while they were transitioning from this life to another. To my cousin Donald R. Tunsil who has constantly requested a copy of this book for the last twenty-five years. And to my entire family—my children, my niece Khyana Pumphrey, and grandchildren who supported me in this endeavor.

A special thank you to the 100 Black men who supported my initial research in role conflict with African American fathers, without their participation I would not have attained my doctorate degree.

A special thank you to the Association of Black Nursing Faculty, Inc. and Chi Eta Phi Sorority, Inc. who permitted access to their membership. A humble thank you for all the nurses who participated in the research on minority nurse role conflict, racism in nursing and the invisible Black nurse. Without their encouragement and willingness to share their story, this book would not exist. This book is dedicated to the nursing profession in all its diversity.

—Ora Valentena (Tena) Robinson

As I embarked on my first book, the intent is to stimulate change, eliminate acts of racism toward Black nurses, minority nurses, and White nurses who have reported reverse racism from other minority groups and create a healing environment for racial reconciliation.

Remember, none of us decided what race, shades of color, hair texture, ethnicity, and family we would belong to.

Were you asked?

Table of Contents

FORWARD

In the essential realms of healthcare and nursing, where empathy and care are fundamental, the story of the Black nurse has too often been marginalized. My unique experiences across nursing, academia, and military service— as a retired Department of Veterans Affairs Chief of Nursing Education and Research, a retired US Army Lt. Colonel, and a Fulbright Scholar—have given me a distinct perspective on our profession's complexities. Like Dr. Ora Robinson, author of "The Invisible Black Nurse," I am a Black nurse who has endured and witnessed the resilience needed to confront workplace and societal racism.

My early education at Little Rock Central High School during desegregation taught me firsthand the systemic injustices that continue to affect our society and professional environments. Many Black nurses, including myself, have faced both covert and overt racism, impacting not only our well-being but also patient care, career advancement, and stress management.

"The Invisible Black Nurse" by Dr. Robinson opens critical discussions on racism within nursing. It calls for a transparent dialogue on racism's effects and is a timely work that illuminates the path toward diversity and inclusion, offering insights from the real experiences of Black nurses. The book invites all nurses to understand the complexities of racism in our profession, highlighting the significant impact of unaddressed racial biases.

Dr. Robinson's journey to publication, spanning nearly three decades, demonstrates the bravery needed to address such a crucial topic. Her work, advocating for social justice, diversity, and inclusion, marks a pivotal step forward. It is a call to acknowledge and listen to Black nurses, fostering a more inclusive and empathetic nursing field that paves the way for healing, understanding, and transformation. "The Invisible Black Nurse" is essential reading for anyone in nursing committed to understanding and changing the dynamics of racism.

Gloria J. Willingham-Toure' PhD, MNSc, BSN

CEO, AframGlobal Organization Inc.

Introduction

If you picked up this book, you may be wondering should I be reading this book? Who is this book for? Yes, this book is for you.

This book is for the Black nurse who expends most of their energy as a professional care provider while combatting acts of intolerance from colleagues, patients, and other members of the health care team.

It is for the Black nurse who spends most of their energy trying to manage their family, confusion, disappointment, anger, and grief as they move through each day

It's for the nurse who finds themselves feeling anxiety that even though they're exhausted, they can't sleep.

It's for the nurse who looks in the eyes of their children and grandchildren and hopes that by the time they enter the workforce, things will be different.

The book is written for all nurses who want to be a change agent to eradicate racial bullying. One nurse verbalized that she goes through her day combatting harassment from patients and from her peers. She goes home exhausted, goes to bed, and starts all over again the next day.

This book is for nurses who experience acts of other "isms" due to their race, ethnicity, and cultural, gender, or sexual orientation.

It is for nurses who want to be empowered to withstand the overt and covert acts of racial incivility and other isms from their peers.

It is for nurses who want to maintain their sanity and improve their mental health, psychological wellbeing, and physical health when experiencing bully behavior from their colleagues.

This book is for those in leadership, mentoring, and coaching roles to help them understand the experiences that Black nurses encounter from their peers daily and their role in mitigating those behaviors that contribute to a toxic work environment.

Leadership can no longer exhibit the "ostrich effect" (denial of existence putting their head in the sand). The leadership has a moral and legal obligation to be proactive in identifying any behavior that falls under the category of harassment specific to race, culture, ethnicity, religious affiliation, sexual orientation, and gender identity and other forms of harassment.

Lastly, this book will benefit those nurses who have engaged in acts of incivility toward other nurses to give them insight into the how these behaviors affect the physical and psychological health of their fellow nurses.

You will gain insight into the day-to-day struggles of "nursing while Black," being under the constant threat of sabotage, being humiliated, and not being respected in their professional roles.

The Benefits of Reading This Book

This book aims to give the reader a glimpse of and to bring awareness and insight on what it's like to be a Black nurse on the frontlines in America.

The Invisible Black Nurse is a collection of behaviors that have been identified synonymous with the terms "bully behavior, incivility, racial bullying, horizontal abuse, horizontal violence, lateral violence, and relational aggression."

Enjoy the journey.

The principles and applications discussed in this book will be beneficial and applicable to individuals in other racial, ethnic, and cultural groups who experience a hostile work environment based on their racial or cultural identity.

You will have opportunities for self-reflection as you will be introduced to "rules of engagement" meaning how to communicate using terms and techniques that are not perceived as wrapped in bias or racism. Take this opportunity to reflect on how your behavior may have impacted others.

The overall "why" of the book is to bring awareness to the experiences that Black nurses encounter while working in their professional role as a registered nurse and to inspire nurses to be a change agent in promoting racial harmony. These experiences adversely impact the physical and mental health, psychological wellbeing, and spiritual health of a person. The good news is that these nurses continued to provide quality care to their patients.

This book presents contemporary research to get a sense of the state of Black registered nurses in America in the 21st century.

Furthermore, it creates a safe environment to engage in self-reflection as you immerse yourself in the stories . The reflection process will help you identify self-care activities, coping strategies, and strategies for perseverance and resilience.

For the non-Black nurse, communication strategies will be discussed from Black nurses who responded to a research question on best practices that would create a supportive communication environment when speaking with Black nurses. Strategies are also given for Black nurses to create a comfortable environment for discourse. Best practices to engage Black nurses/women is using assertive communication (care confrontation) and strategies to create a trusting environment. Faith-based strategies are incorporated to help find your voice. It is vital to have a safe place for racial discourse.

You will be introduced to the syndrome of invisibility (horizontal abuse/ scrutinization/de-legitimization of the professional role), and identify factors that lead to resilience, perseverance, health consequences of unforgiveness, health benefits of forgiveness, lessons learned, and rules of engagement.

Where do we go from here?

Become immersed in the physical and psychological health effects through the stories of others.

Health promotion activities will be shared to mitigate the physical and psychological effects of being invisible, or you could say, "ignored in plain sight." Black women who are assertive speak their mind, practice direct communication, and make eye contact are put into the categories of the "angry Black women" , "the angry Black nurse" or the "bitchy" nurse.

Awaken your inner spirit to become a change agent. Fear will turn to faith, and anger to forgiveness.

Be empowered to participate in the discussion on issues around race and the challenges of "nursing while Black" under extreme working conditions in clinical , academic administrative, and research roles.

A synopsis of select research will be shared to facilitate racial reconciliation within the nursing profession, moving toward racial civility in nursing. The shared stories will be cathartic for both the nurse receiving bullying and the nurse who is demonstrating bullying behaviors.

Racial Reconciliation

This book will move the reader toward racial reconciliation with nurses of color—specifically Black nurses. The first step in the healing process is the awareness that there is a problem. We can no longer engage in the ostrich effect. The reader will become empathetic to the actual experiences of "nursing while Black." Be transformed, as you walk in the shoes of your Black peers through their stories. Fully experience their journey of pain, frustration, and resilience.

For example, Black nurses are constantly bombarded with being asked if they are the housekeeper or the nursing assistant. One nurse, a research participant, stated, "They see me in a white uniform, name tag with the letters RN, and they ask me if I'm the housekeeper."

Understand that a safe environment has been created for you to reflect on your ability to be empathetic toward your Black colleagues and reflect on the possibility of how you may have contributed to their pain and frustration.

As you proceed, you go through each section, you will engage and discover your comfort level when reading the stories. For example, if you are uneasy reading these stories through the words on the page, it may mirror your discomfort to engage in dialogue face-to-face. I encourage you to pause, reflect, and meditate on lessons learned while also focusing on how to incorporate the principles in your personal and professional life.

Upon completion of this book, you will have heightened awareness of the challenges Black nurses experience in their day-to-day role as a registered nurse. In addition, you will gain insight on how to create a workplace that is psychologically safe for Black nurses, and non-Black nurses to stop the phenomenon of nurses eating their young and promote civility amongst all nurses.

Thank you for taking this journey.

About the Author

Let me introduce myself. My humble beginnings began in Lake City Florida, the gateway to Florida. I am the second of five children—four ladies and one gentleman. Although I was a shy child, my imagination was always beyond the stars. I have very early memories of wanting to make a difference on this earth—to stop wars and promote peace. As a child, I did not realize that was a tall order. Mother said I was content to sit in a box and watch the other kids play. I was not very interactive with other kids and was happy being in solitude.

My nursing career started late in life after being discouraged by a teacher at community college who never called upon me in class when I raised my hand. You may wonder… *why quit?* I had other experiences that told me what I could not become and directed me to courses I already had competencies from high school. My response was to quit school.

I have written this book with over 40 years of experience in the health care field. My nursing journey has expanded over 25 years ranging from community colleges, universities, post-secondary colleges, private institutions of nursing, and vocational nursing programs. My personal mission is to inspire, motivate, and educate others to meet their goals. This led to my passion for impacting social change within the nursing profession by eradicating racial bullying and the phenomenon of nurses eating their young.

"ISMS"

Description: Phase one describes the "isms" that are encountered in nursing by Black registered nurses in the clinical and academic settings. Examples of select isms will give insight into how Black nurses experience these behaviors from peers. The Webster Dictionary defines the word "peer" as "one that is of equal standing with another." One belonging to the same societal group—in this case, the societal group are nurses. "Colleague" is defined as "an associate in a profession." "Collegial" is defined as "equal sharing of authority and collegiality, the cooperative relationship of colleagues." Therefore, the term "peer" will be used to denote the relationship between nurses. and vocational nursing programs. My personal mission is to inspire, motivate, and educate others to meet their goals. This led to my passion for impacting social change within the nursing profession by eradicating racial bullying and the phenomenon of nurses eating their young.

Chapter 1

Racism

Although the book is about Black nurses and their invisibility, there are other groups that experience some form of isms based on their ethnicity, culture, gender identity, sexual orientation, age, and religion. Americans has always looked through the lens of White and Black.

What are isms? When you look up "ism" in the dictionary, it talks about one having an ethnocentric approach to others who do not fit into their racial or ethnic group that are the receivers of the dominant group who feels superior over others. There are many types of isms that one may experience. For example, we have racism which means being discriminated based on one's race. We have colorism based on the color spectrum of light to dark shades of Black. Black male nurses have also verbalized that they are treated differently by their White peers. We also have ageism— prejudice and discrimination toward another based on their age.

I experienced the burden of ageism as a 17-year-old high school graduate who could not secure employment due to age. In the 50's, I watched younger peers move up the career ladder. In the 60's, I discovered we are looked at through the lens of how much expense we will cause the organization through illness or retirement rather than the caliber of our mind and our experience. Let me offer a visual tour of what this experience looks like.

I have experienced a combination of racism and sexism when working with predominantly White men in the medical profession. Many expect you to be docile and passive. Black women are not docile or passive—not by choice, but by necessity. We are accused of being aggressive when we speak up for ourselves versus being seen as assertive. On the negative, we are seen as the "Black Bitch."

In our training as nurses, we are trained to be assertive, speak in an active voice, and to be a patient advocate through our voice. We are trained to question physicians about orders if they do not seem appropriate for the patient. We use our critical thinking skills and clinical reasoning skills to analyze the data and derive conclusions based on that data. Some White men are not accustomed to being challenged by women—in particularly, Black women.

For some reason, I am not fearful of White men unless they are pointing a weapon at me. You will read later in the book about an experience I had when a White man stood over me in an aggressive stance and how I responded. In my role as a registered nurse, I am not afforded the opportunity to fear White men as majority of the physicians I worked with are White men.

Oh, it gets better. My sexual orientation has been questioned based on my choice of clothes and how I wear my hair—or lack of it. Let me share another visual of nursing while Black.

4

I recall a time when I was at a clinical facility and saw the director coming in my direction. Her face was in the "resting bitch mode" as the young people call it. I could hear the pitter patter of her high heels walking fast toward me. The director did a hard stop and blurted out, "The residents may not want you to care for them as they may think you are gay."

Wow! She blurted it out like that in front of the students. I thought to myself, okay, it's because of how I look. That was the first thing that came to mind. It was my race. That's the first thing people see. Now, let me add gay to the list.

I had no idea what I was about to hear from this director in front of my students, but I did not expect this behavior. The director went on to say because my hair was shaved, the residents may think I was gay. She stood there in a stoic position, awaiting a response.

How do you respond? I said, "Okay, I hear you. That will not be a problem." She stood silently looking at me again with no response. Again, I stated that it will not be a problem. Finally, I said to myself, let me calm this director down.

I reiterated that would be no problem because I have a drawer full of wigs. I explained that I can easily put a wig on when at this clinical site. "Will that work for you?" Our eyes locked and I didn't blink. She turned around and walked off, not a response, not anything.

I tried to schedule an appointment with her prior to the clinical assignment and she never responded. That is the reason I would like to meet with the directors to see what their expectations are to avoid any humiliation upon arriving.

That's an example that I never thought I would experience in terms of being denied caring for somebody based on the assumption that I was gay or because of my shaved hair.

My students were in awe and felt bad for me. Pause. How do I respond to the students? I gave my speech about nurses being adaptable and the need to maintain our clinical affiliations. In addition, I'm not willing to expend my energy on ignorance.

The director demonstrated no empathy. There was no consideration given as to whether I was a cancer survivor or if it were my first day relinquishing wigs to wear my baldness proudly, or if I had self-esteem issues, or even perhaps experiencing any health condition that would cause hair loss.

I told my students, "In life, you must select what battles to fight. Select only those battles you know that will work toward winning the war. This battle would not move the needle to end the war on racism."

Take some time to reflect on this situation and write down your thoughts and feelings:

Lessons Learned:

_____

_____

_____

_____

On sexism...

I was sitting at my desk in the back of the building which is isolated from the main offices. Visualize walking down a long hall—about two city blocks. When you get to the end, make a left turn, and walk 300 feet to my office.

Because of the location, I usually lock the door, but this one time, I didn't as I put down my belongings on the desk. There were only two doors to the exit. As I placed my purse on the filing cabinet and my backpack under the desk, I sat down to prepare for the day. I notified the front office I was on campus and asked if my 10 a.m. appointment was here. The answer was no.

As I sat at my desk looking down at my appointment book, I heard the doorknob turn. He did not knock on the door. He opened the door and just came in. I could hear his hard shoes landing on the floor in a hard cadence.

I could smell the odor of his breath which wasn't too appealing. (In my mind I was thinking, get the fudge sickle out of my face, back the fudge up). This was prior to my recommitment to using fruits of the spirit and having words that edify others come out of my mouth.

As I looked up, I saw this big burly man (the interim department chair, non-nurse) walk toward my desk. Our eyes locked and before I could stand up, he put his hands on my desk and leaned over. I heard a rough voice say, "We don't think you can teach. You would be best suited in administration." (I was wondering who "we" were). As I maintained eye contact with him, you could hardly put a hand's width between his mouth and my face. You may be thinking, weren't you scared? As a psychiatric nurse and a person who grew up in the inner city, I learned to control my responses of being scared to stay focused. Besides, I'm not easily intimidated.

Upon reflection, I should have picked up the phone and asked security to come to my office. He had to be at least 6'4' and over 240 lbs. As a psychiatric nurse, I should have stood up to be at his eye level, but I opted to stay put. I removed one of my hands from the desk and fumbled through my purse that was in the desk drawer to locate my pepper spray. I was intrigued by his posture, but I maintained eye contact.

I would advise any person to call security immediately and not take it upon yourself. I looked at him and said, "You have missed the deadline to talk about my teaching abilities. This meeting is for you to orient me on the director's role for this campus.

You missed that opportunity when you did not respond to my rebuttal." (How can a non-nurse evaluate my teaching effectiveness when he knows nothing about nursing and had not visited my classroom?!) Looking directly in his eyes, I told him to have a seat. He looked at me, backed up, and positioned his arms across his chest and sat down. Pause.

What are your thoughts? Take a minute to write them down on the space below:

_____

_____

_____

_____

_____

_____

_____

I responded, "Okay, let's proceed talking about the reason for the meeting: reviewing role expectations of the director." I had requested a formal meeting in the form of a rebuttal to respond to my questions regarding how I did not meet the criteria for tenure and promotion when the department and the university recommended advancement for tenure and promotion.

(I went home to my father's funeral and upon return, I was banished from the main campus which is 15 minutes from my home, and I was sent to the campus one hour away. He did not offer condolences at any time prior to leaving or upon return).

Now anyone who has lost their parents knows that this is not a good time to get on someone's nerves. I just buried my daddy who loved my mother for 64 years and taught his girls how a man should treat a woman. I was thinking, what would my daddy tell me to do? He would say don't get dragged in the bull crap. Whereas my mother would say, leave the job and do your own thing. I'm glad I had more of my daddy's disposition.

I had access to my pepper spray if he made another aggressive move. You may be thinking, what pepper spray? Yes, our campus held safety courses for students and faculty to defend themselves from any threat that would cause bodily harm. In addition, I took a self-defense class on campus, therefore, I knew how to bring him down.

But why should I be put in a position as a leader to be subjected to this type of behavior in the workplace? Why should I have to defend myself against someone who is familiar with my leadership role? But the whisper of my daddy and the Father said "Be still and know that I am God. I will take care of him."

Can you think of any isms that you have experienced? Take a minute and self-reflect on this story. How did it make you feel? Write down a few thoughts:

_____

_____

_____

_____

_____

_____

_____

Those of you who have engaged in bully behaviors toward the isms, write down how it made you feel. For example, did you feel empowered, authoritative, or satisfied?

_____

_____

_____

_____

_____

_____

_____

On racism…

In the 1828 Webster Dictionary, the terms "racism" and "nigger" were not yet defined. The term "Negro" described "an individual as a native or descendant of the Black race of men in Africa who was quite Black but not the tawny or olive colored in the northern coast of Africa." (Webster Dictionary, 1828.) "Negress" was referred to as "the female of the Black race of Africa." The Latin spelling was "niger." The Latin pronunciation was "nee-gur." I began to wonder at what point the pronunciation evolved into a derogatory term.

Upon review of Merriam-Webster 2020, racism is defined as "a belief that race is the primary determinant of human traits and capacities and that racial difference produce an inherent superiority of a particular race." The term denotes racial prejudice or discrimination. I looked up "negro" which was described as "sometimes offensive"— "a member of the humankind native to Africa and classified according to physical features such as dark skin pigmentation (Merriam-

Webster, 2020). The term "negroness" replaced "negress" and was identified as sometimes offensive. I then went on to see if the "N word" was defined.

The N word was there described as an alteration of the early term "niger/neger." It was used as an "insult and contemptuous term for a member of any dark-skinned race" who is systematically subjected to discrimination and unfair treatment. It went on to describe it as a racial slur. As I reflect on the definition, and look at my brown skin, am I not a "N word?" When used by non-Black people, it is an expression of pure contempt for that race of people.

Lastly, I wanted to see how other countries viewed the terms negro and the N word. It was not used in other countries. The recurring theme of the meaning was "that of Black and those of dark skin." It is also noteworthy that its being offensive depended on the countries and regions it was being used in. To discuss the different definitions for each country and region would be too exhaustive for this book. Therefore, a snapshot view was given in the book to frame the discussion on "racism in nursing" in America. The stories you will read will depict a recurring theme of systematic prejudice, discrimination, and those going out of their way to impede the profession of the negro, negress, African American and Black nurses.

INVISIBILITY
The Research

Jeremiah 12:3

As for you Lord, You know me; You see me…

Chapter 2

Being Invisible:
The Research

P hase Two describes the historical and contemporary research on Black registered nurses. It gives a comparison of historical and contemporary research on Black registered nurses. Historical and contemporary research will introduce the phenomenon of "The Invisible Black Nurse."

Systemic racism in nursing is discussed based on the statistics of Blacks who are represented in nursing, through the admission of nursing students, and those in their professional role of the nursing faculty. Inference of systemic racism is made based on the statistical analysis of entry into practice.

Stories of being invisible are shared by Black registered nurses from staff nurses, clinical nurse specialists, nurse educators in academia, nurse administrators, and nursing students. Select book reviews are presented in a chronological approach to bring awareness to the reader in the lack of change that has occurred over a time frame from the 1800s to 21st century. Select nursing research and parallel research are reviewed as well. Recurring recommendations are included to disseminate this research as a point of discussion.

Historical Perspectives

Historically, during the era of segregation, the nursing profession has excluded Black nurses as equal partners in the delivery of health care. White nurses during that time had less than favorable views of Black nurses. For example, many White undergraduate nurses believe that Black nurses had inferior intelligence as evidenced by poor judgment, limited intellectual capacity, and their responsibility. This type of opinion was supported by research that implied that the brain of the Black man was smaller with limited capacity for intellectual thought. This was in alignment with the pathological theory that Blacks' brains were smaller than Whites,' therefore, being less intelligent.

The historical perspective is offered as a synopsis to frame the discussion as an ongoing problem from a historical perspective and what is currently happening in the 21st century. Come join me as we reflect on whence we came and where are we going.

Black Women in White: Racial Conflict and Cooperation in the Nursing Profession, 1890-1950 was written by Darlene Clark Hine. The first edition was published in 1989. She looked at the institutional infrastructure of nursing and racism, status, and the professionalization of nursing. She speaks about "We Shall Not Be Left Out" as it relates to the integration of Black nurses during World War II. She brought out the issue of racial antipathy and class divisions. White nurse leaders excluded Black nurses and adopted exclusionary policies and practices that rendered Black nurses' professional outcasts. As a result, the National Association of Colored Graduate Nurses was formed. She chronicled the relentless struggle of Black nurses and their leaders trying to integrate into mainstream American nursing. This struggle continues today.

Carnegie (1986, 1995, 2000), *The Path We Tread: Blacks in Nursing Worldwide*, looked at the contributions of Black nurses over a time span from 1854-1990 which shows the relevancy of this topic in the 21st century. The book won two awards from the American Academy of Nursing for positive portrayal of nurses and the other from the American Journal of Nursing as book of the year. The discussion spans the Crimean, Civil, and the Spanish-American War. The discussion on the "struggle for recognition" was powerful as people showcased their accomplishments in organizations that originally did not welcome nurses of color. The power of the book is the photos of those people who broke these barriers and contributed to the health of their respective nations.

In addition, some White people believed that Black nurses could not manage the aspects of management and lacked the executive skills required to perform the responsibilities of a leader. Furthermore, it was believed that Black nurses could not withstand the pressures in a hospital setting. In summary, Black nurses were considered to have weak character, limited intelligence, and having no morals. Therefore, Black nurses were not included in the professional organizations and were relegated to the care of only the Black community. As nurses, they could not work on White patients. Their experience came from hospitals designated as Black.

Does this sound familiar? The same analogy of the water fountain in the south that says, "Whites only fountain." I remember as a kid, I asked my cousins, "Is there a difference in the water? The water doesn't look Black."

As I reflected on the above statement, I took a pause, sighed, and said, "Lord have mercy." Those thoughts were as far back from the 1800's to the 1950's. I could feel the tension in my shoulders as I reflected on how not much has changed as these thoughts are still prevalent among some of our White peers and other nurses of color. It is disheartening, seeing that in the nursing profession. whose motto is caring for others. while at the same time seeing that they do not demonstrate that same level of caring for one another.

Exclusion continued well into the 21st century and has caused some Black nurses to experience feelings of ambiguity when implementing their professional role responsibilities. The Black nurse have participated in the American dream, which says, "If you work hard, play by the rules, get an education. you can be successful. You can have a piece of the American pie." We are still searching for that piece of pie.

As I reflect on the rich history of Blacks in nursing, I can't quit. I can't stop researching and documenting these stories of perseverance and hope. Why?

Because Harriet Tubman did not quit as she risked her life and those of others to get to the promised land up north. Darlene Clark Hine did not quit as she wrote on racial conflict and cooperation and the nursing profession during the period of 1890 to 1950.

Mary Elizabeth Carnegie did not quit as she wrote *The Path we Tread, Blacks in Nursing Worldwide*. Mary Mahoney, the first Black nurse did not quit, and other unsung heroes who fought for equality. Therefore, I write, The Invisible Black Nurse.

There continues to be scant literature on evidence methods to intervene to stop the cycle of racial bullying and horizontal abuse of Black nurses by their caring colleagues. Contemporary books have addressed the problem behavior as incivility, vertical or lateral abuse, bullying, and toxicity within nursing.

There is no evidence that specifically addresses the bullying received by Black nurses based on their racial category. Black nurses feel invisible because of not being acknowledged in their professional role (de-legitimization of the professional role), when they are held to higher standards than their peers (scrutinization), and bully behavior as a function of their racial identity.

For example, I experienced this phenomenon when sitting at a round table with seven of my colleagues and a candidate for an assistant professor. The chair of the recruitment committee proceeded to introduce the faculty sitting at the round table. Imagine being the candidate when you hear the introductions as follows:

This is Dr. A, Dr. B, Dr. C. Dr. C., Ora, Dr. D, Dr. E, and Dr. F.

The White candidate immediately gave me eye contact and her nonverbal expression was priceless as she tried to keep a straight face and not let her frown show through.

You may be wondering at this point how I responded. No response showed her ignorance as it was blatant. I reflected on the following scriptures:

Proverbs 26:4

*"Answer not a fool according to his folly,
lest thou also be like unto him."*

Psalms 141:3

*"Set a watch, O Lord, before my mouth:
keep the door of my lips."*

I opted not to say anything at that point. Why would I contribute to unprofessional and blatant prejudicial behavior in front of everyone? I opted to reflect on two scriptural verses:

Luke 6:45

"A good man out of the good treasure of his heart brings forth good; and an evil man out of the evil treasure of his heart brings forth evil. For out of

the abundance of the heart his mouth speaks."

I had suspected she had some sort of feeling about me, based on her behavior toward me and putting others in positions I was next in line for. But I do not make it a habit to call the race card by default. The next scripture I thought of was:

Proverbs 3:9

"Do not speak in the hearing of a fool, for he will despise the wisdom of your words."

I had to train myself not to respond to foolishness, because if I did, then I would have also become a fool. Everyone sitting at that table knew that was weird because those who were chewing stopped and just looked in awe, awaiting my response.

The candidate caught me as I was leaving and verbalized her frustration and disgust at the exchange. The candidate went on to say that after this behavior, she was no longer interested in working in an environment that is outwardly prejudiced. I said nothing, smiled, and wished her continued success in her journey.

> *This is one overt example of "delegitimization of the professional role." Black nurses experience overt and covert acts of racism. For example, those that have attained terminal degrees are not acknowledged with that designation—they are communicated to as if they were "the help."*

Lessons learned: Do not expend your energy on fools.

In addition, there is no evidence on the adverse health consequences that Black nurses experience because of a constant menu of racial bullying.

Take a pause and write your thoughts on this exchange.

Chapter 3

Contemporary Research Perspectives

This chapter evolved out of 20 years of research— both historical and contemporary that allowed me to listen to others relive their stories and share their internal and external conflicts. The storyteller's demeanor goes back in time, and you can see the pain on their faces and the agitation that emerges from their body language. Some of them recounted their stories as if it happened just yesterday.

My intent is to disseminate information on the plight of Blacks in nursing and stimulate change to eliminate acts of racial bullying by their peers from White and non-Black minority groups. Although the discussion is on the racism experienced by other non-Black nurses, there is in-group racism based on shades of color (colorism). There is a growing trend of reverse racism toward White nurses who have reported reverse racism from other minority groups.

Nurses are trained to be advocates and change agents. Let's be the change to show others how to "get along without going it alone."

We have looked at the historical experiences of nursing while Black. Now let's look at how far we have come. We can agree that Black nurses were not afforded the same opportunities. Let's look at the NLN graphics on Minorities and Faculty in nursing programs.

Graphic I. Percentage of Minorities in Basic RN Programs by Race-Ethnicity, 2018

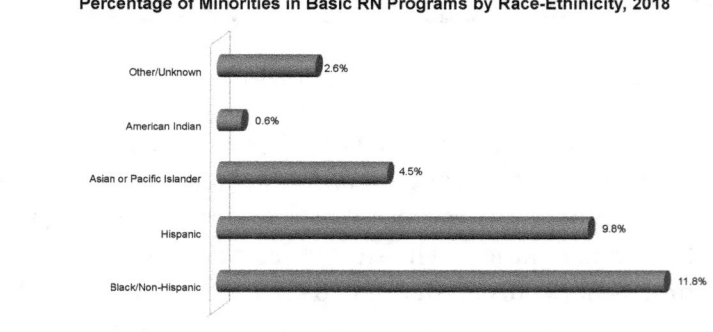

Percentage of Minorities in Basic RN Programs by Race-Ethinicity, 2018

National League for Nursing Biennial Survey of Schools of Nursing, 2018

The graphs depict the percentage of minorities in RN programs, but there is no percentage of Whites in these programs.

Graphic II: Distribution Full-time Nurse Educators by Race, 2019.

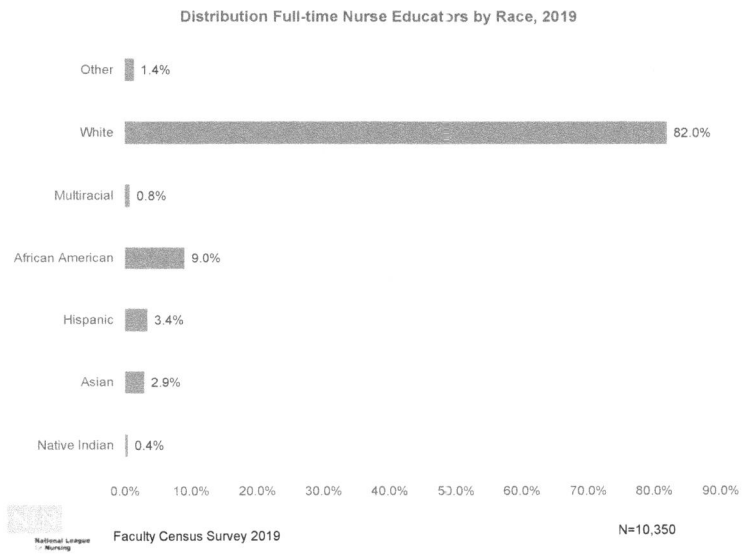

Distribution Full-time Nurse Educators by Race, 2019

Race	Percentage
Other	1.4%
White	82.0%
Multiracial	0.8%
African American	9.0%
Hispanic	3.4%
Asian	2.9%
Native Indian	0.4%

Faculty Census Survey 2019   N=10,350

You can see from the graph that there is a gap of full-time Black faculty compared to that of White nursing faculty. Take a minute. reflect and pause. Write down your thoughts below:

Let's take a closer look at what has been said in contemporary research in this area. The focus is on books in the marketplace that have addressed the general challenges of the nursing profession. These have been well received. The stories presented in these texts have been engaging and include a research component to validate the stories being told by nurses.

For the reader who is not a nurse, the nursing profession has a phenomenon of "eating their young." This translates into not offering support for new nurses coming into the field. This non-support has morphed into terms like incivility, bullying, relational aggression, and racial bullying. These books not only discuss the problem but offer solutions to the problems.

The difference between their titles and the title of this book is the emphasis on race as a phenomenon of nurses "eating their young." I have lived these experiences. Other nurses who identify as Black, have mirrored similar experiences, feelings, behaviors, and negative health consequences.

Hearing their stories brought tears to my eyes as they took me back on their journey. I observed their countenance change, and their pain hurt as they recounted their story. Their eyes watered up as if they were experiencing the event for the first time. Because of this, I conducted research to comprehend the physical and psychological effects of observed racial bullying of nursing students.

Prior evidence-based articles titles have not focused on Black nurses and the negative health consequences they encounter because of racial bullying. Unpublished research (Robinson, 2009) examined the physical and psychological effects of nursing students' experiences of racism in the clinical and academic settings. Impedance cardiography was used to measure the physiologic responses of participants when responding to a series of questions concerning their experiences with racism in the clinical and academic setting. Non-verbal responses were captured using the Facial Action Coding System (FACS) to identify facial changes while responding to the questions. Changes were identified from the participants' neutral facial position and classified as action units. Table I shows the survey questions asked.

Table I Survey Questions

1.	What is the first word that comes to mind when you think about racism?
2.	How would you define racism?
3.	List adjectives that come to mind when you think about role conflict.
4.	How do you define nurse role conflict?
5.	Have you observed acts of racism in the clinical setting?
6.	How did that make you feel?
7.	Which one of the following most reflects how you felt when you experienced or observed acts of racism (angry, sad, confused, anxiety)?
8.	Have you experienced in-group racism—defined as racism from within your own racial, ethnic, or cultural group?
9.	Have you experienced acts of racism toward you from nursing staff during your clinical rotation?
10.	Have you experienced perceived acts of racism from nursing faculty?

11.	Have you demonstrated any acts of racism toward others?
12.	Have you observed acts of racism toward patients while in the clinical setting?
13.	How would you describe behavioral characteristics of acts of racism toward others that you have observed while in the clinical setting?
14.	What type of behavior do you associate with acts of racism?
15.	Can you describe your behavioral responses when imparting acts of racism toward others?
16.	Can you identify the type of behavior you displayed while experiencing acts of racism?
17.	Can you describe any physical responses to observed or experienced acts of racism during the clinical rotation?
18.	Which of the following best describes your physiologic responses and psychological responses to acts of racism?
19.	Which of the following best describes your behavioral responses to acts of racism (anger, harming others, using vulgarity, becoming mute, harming self)?
20.	Do you feel you are held to a higher standard of learning based on your race?
21.	Do you feel invisible based on your race while in the clinical setting?
22.	Do you feel that perceived experiences with racism contributes to health disparities among minority students?
23.	What racial group do you feel has a higher incidence of perceived acts of racism against them?

24.	Do you consider yourself a person who demonstrates acts of racism toward others? (yes, no, not sure, sometimes)
25.	Do your experiences with racism interfere with your ability to learn?
26.	Do your experiences with racism interfere with your ability to deliver patient care?

Still I Rise

Did you want to see me broken? Bowed head and lowered eyes? Shoulders falling down like teardrops, weakened by my soulful cries... You may shoot me with your

words, you may cut me with your eyes, you may kill me with your hatefulness, but still, like air, I'll rise.

—*Maya Angelou*

Gupta (2009) looked at racism in nursing and laid out the foundation of why it is important to study racism in nursing. She described an incidence experienced by a nurse in Ontario, Canada. The nurse was fired, and she filed a complaint that she has been a victim of racial harassment and unfair treatment due to her color. She was held to a higher standard than her peers. She was put on suspension for being late, followed around by her nurse manager, and her nursing practice was under constant scrutinization. She was accused of many things including yelling.

The author mentioned the point that these nurses are not believed in the legal system and compared it to a woman being raped—who is also not believed. Black nurses are viewed as guilty until proven innocent.

Another discussion deals with Black nurses' complaints being viewed as exaggerated, or that they are playing the race card. They are also accused of having a chip on their shoulder.

The book looks at racism in the Canadian context with workplace racial harassment. Black nurses are asked to report on other Black nurses to be used to their detriment. The objective of the book was to describe the common experiences, patterns, features, and surface manifestations of systemic racism in nursing in Ontario, and the second was to build a theoretical framework for understanding systematic racism.

The author also found evidence of reverse racism in White nurses who experienced racism from other nationalities. She goes on to say that racism requires social power, therefore reverse racism is a contradiction in terms. Power is described not on an individual basis but based on the product of group power as social rather than at the individual level. Therefore, their ability to make decisions benefit their group. There is historical evidence that racism by Whites represents a continuation of White supremacy in many societies.

Dellasega (2011) looked at the cycle of bullying, when nurses hurt nurses, and recognizing and overcoming the cycle of bullying. She framed the discussion in terms of relational aggression among adolescents who grow up as adults. Nursing, being a predominantly female profession have inherent bias based on being female and how they manage relationships. She speaks of the "mean girl" syndrome and use the term "female bullying." Additional content is given on tools of the trade of bullies which include gossip, exclusion, disloyalty, humiliation, manipulation, and intimidation.

Gutierrez y Muhs et. al. (2012) looked at the intersection of race and class titled Presumed Incompetent: The Intersections of Race and Class for Women in Academia. The authors give a comprehensive review and discussion of the experiences of faculty of color. Their overarching premise is that there is a contradictory culture of academia that purports to welcome free speech and diversity of truth, yet faculty of color are not afforded that same truth. The book is comprised of a collection of essays that show social hierarchies that pervade American society including race, gender, class, and sexuality.

Threat (2015) explored nursing civil rights as it relates to gender and race in the army nurse corps. One of her profound statements was the negro nurse fighting for democracy. She also talks about how White men in nursing have complicated the issue by pushing the boundaries of racial discrimination based on being in a female dominated profession. The book gives a complex view of the paths of discrimination faced by Black nurses and White men in nursing.

Ciocco (2018) presented an extensive discussion on combating nurse bullying, incivility, and workplace violence. She draws on the ANA Code of ethics that state nurses are required to "Create an ethical environment and culture of civility and kindness, treating colleagues, coworkers, employees, students, and others with dignity and respect" (ANA, 2015, p.4).

However, the sad truth is this does not occur when working with peers. The book explores bully behavior across the spectrum from students to leadership. She looks at the cost of bully behavior and the impact it has on the health care systems. She also looks at the global phenomenon of bullying in nursing.

Leymann (1996) identified the effects bullying has on an individual which includes communication, maintaining social contacts, maintaining personal reputation, poor performance and physical health concerns. The book defines incivility and discusses the relationship between incivility and stress. It identifies ten uncivil behaviors, five effects of incivility on the nursing profession, and individual and organizational strategies to mitigate incivility. There is a section on the need to change nursing education as they allow bullying behaviors in academia. Bully behavior ranging from the student nurse to the faculty and colleagues against colleagues.

As you can see, the information is given in reverse chronological order to see the progression and continuation of this subject matter. Dellasega (2019) continued her discussion on how to understand and resolve relational aggression and strategies to deal with relational aggression and bullying.

Dellasega asks the following questions:

- ✓ "Are nurses caring or cruel?
- ✓ How can they switch off their behavior from kindness to being mean toward their colleagues?"

What do you think? What experiences have you had or observed?

_____

_____

_____

_____

_____

There has been a robust reporting of bully type behaviors, but minimal discussion on how Black nurses experience racial bullying and the health consequences. . Black nurses experience adverse consequences of racial bullying in their physical, emotional, and psychological health.

An emerging finding from the research was feeling like an outsider. This contributed to feelings of loneliness, social isolation, alienation, and feeling invisible. One participant stated:

"I have been here for five years and there is nobody that I can truly call a friend that just comes to the office and talks to me and just sits down and asks me, 'How are you doing?' as a person. It is a very lonely position."

Additional themes revolved around unequal access to resources that would help with promotion and tenure, limiting access to resources and insincerity. One participant stated:

"Because I learned one day that all three of us faculty of color [FoC] had the same feeling that we couldn't trust anybody, that we couldn't have these kinds of conversations with folks about: how do you get ahead? How do you get tenure here? They would have been going up before I would have been going up. But we were all completely ignorant about that process. So, I began to believe that there was some systematic process in place—institutionalized in a way—to keep us quiet so that we would never make it there."

I can relate to the previous statement, as I was denied promotion and tenure twice, once at a community college and the other at the university level. While at the community college level, I was told I would be better suited at the university level. At the university level, I was told I was better suited to be in administration. It is interesting as an older adult how everyone has an opinion of where you should be and makes every effort to make sure you are not successful in meeting your personal or professional goals.

Chapter 4

The Syndrome of Invisibility

The framework of Hardy and Conway (1978) role theory was selected to guide the study of The Invisible Black Nurse. Black Americans have endured and adapted to different labeling categories over the years. For example, we were once negroes, colored, Afro-American (a hair style) Black and most recently, a hyphenated American, i.e., African American.

Role theory identifies roles as ascribed or achieved. The ascribed role includes genetic characteristics which they have no control over, for example, height, eye color, and blood type.

The achieved role includes accomplishments which is attained through education, for example, nursing, attorneys, educators, and musicians

Findings concluded Black nurses are viewed in their ascribed role (race), versus their achieved role (registered nurse).

Let's look at what other researchers have added to the discussion. Stanley (2006) writes on the experiences of faculty of color in predominantly White institutions. She speaks on the phenomenon of racial battle fatigue that leads to race-related stress. The following excerpt from a Black male psychiatric professor's response to the question is profound:

> *"What is it like to be Black in White America today? One step from suicide! It's a wonder we haven't all gone out and killed somebody or killed ourselves"* (Stanley, 2006, p. 315).

Take a minute and reflect on this statement. Use the space below to write down your thoughts, feelings, and any physical changes you experience.

_____

_____

_____

_____

_____

_____

_____

This section will discuss the phenomenon of being held to a higher standard than their peers (scrutinization), being devalued in their achieved role as a professional registered nurse (de-legitimization of the professional role) and being abused by their peers in the form of incivility, relational aggression, mistreatment, sabotage, and racial bullying (horizontal abuse).

In my research, I labeled the actions as horizontal abuse based on no battery resulted from the abuse. I opted not to use the term horizontal violence as it denotes a violent act toward another.

Black nurses are experiencing an increase in uncaring behaviors from their nurse peers. Black nurses have been in the shadows of nursing since the beginning of the nursing profession. There is a deep history of bias, prejudice, and racism toward Black nurses which is well documented in historical and contemporary literature. Exclusion continues to be the plight of the Black nurse.

As we chip away at the glass ceiling, we are met with a layer of concrete, and we start the process over again. We chip away at the concrete ceiling only to meet another layer of BS. We can see the flickering of light and we are met with reinforced layers of BS. White women must deal with breaking the glass where we must deal with breaking the concrete .

Resilience is in our DNA, and we will continue to break the ceilings in whatever form to make it better for the next generations of Black nurses.

At the time of writing, the concrete ceiling was broken when a Black female was elected as the Vice President of the United States. But there is still work to be done. We can't take our foot off the gas.

You do see us—the beauty of our uniqueness, the diversity in our shades of color, our diverse hair texture and styles and our baldness.

How do I know you see me?

- When you go to the tanning booth, you see me.

- When you tan out in the sun on the beach, you see me.

- When you get lip injections in your lips to expand them, you see me.

- When you get buttock implants, you see me.

- When you lay next to your Black man, you see me.

The questions in my initial research were as follows:

- ✓ **"Why** do Black nurses and Black nursing students experience role conflict in the form of perceived racism from their colleagues and peers?"

- ✓ **"Why** are Black nursing students hindered from opportunities to access the research and resources to meet their learning objectives in the clinical setting?"

- ✓ **"Why** do administrators hinder Black professional nurses from progressing in their careers?"

Look at a **figure one**, it reflects the Black nurse experiences with role stress because of their racial category (ascribed role) which they were predestined with at birth. For example, your race, your gender, culture, and ethnicity. This bombardment of stress leads to role strain in their achieved role as a registered nurse. Some Black nurses struggle with self-esteem issues by not being accepted in their achieved role. Because of my solid foundation of who I am, I did not experience self-esteem issues.

Research on the specifics of racism within the nursing profession has not been examined comprehensively. Most of the literature examines race under the context of discrimination, bias, bigotry, culture diversity, and cultural competence. Terms such as discrimination, bias, and bigotry were used to described incidences of racism from 2001-2006 as compared to terms such as disenfranchise, feeling invisible, horizontal violence, lateral violence, and horizontal abuse.

The gap in the literature was evident as there were few articles that used the term racism from the perspective of the Black nurse. The purpose of the research was to identify role conflict experienced as a registered nurse. The hypothesis was Black nurses were viewed based on their ascribed role (race, ethnicity) which they can't change, versus their achieved role (occupation, profession, credentials, etc.).

Figure 1: Emerging graphic depiction of racial incivility

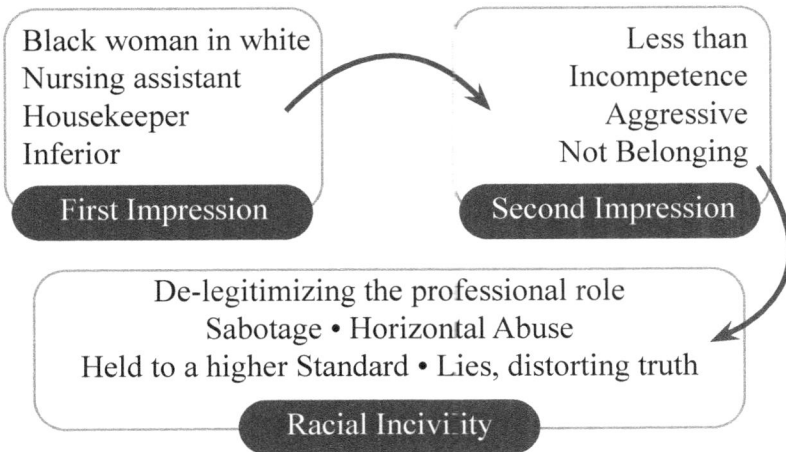

Chapter 5

Narratives to Research Questions

The questions were: (1) Why do Black nurses and Black nursing students encounter role conflict in the form of perceived racism from their colleagues and peers? and (2) Why are Black nursing students hindered from opportunities to access resources to meet their learning objectives in the clinical and academic setting, compared to their White peers?

Role theory identifies roles as ascribed or achieved. The ascribed role includes genetic characteristics which they have no control over, for example, , height, eye color, and blood type.

The achieved role includes accomplishments which is attained through education, for example, nursing, attorneys, educators, and musicians

Findings concluded Black nurses are viewed in their ascribed role (race), versus their achieved role (registered nurse).

The recurring theme was that Black nurses based on first impressions were viewed within the context of their race. This caused them to experience role-related stress. Black nurses were then viewed on the second impression based on their achieved role as a professional registered nurse. These experiences lead to role strain. The experiences of role stress and role strain cumulated into role conflict. Therefore, this phenomenon was referred to as "minority nurse role conflict." The nurses had to balance their ascribed role (race) with their achieved role (RN) while nursing while Black.

The recurring themes were scrutinization (being held to a higher standard), de-legitimization of the professional role (devaluing the role as a RN), and horizontal abuse (receiving behaviors of incivility, lateral violence, relational aggression, and racial bullying).

The stories I am about to share will take you into the world of Black nurses who encounter racism not only from patients but by their peer group of nurses. These stories came from survey evidence, anecdotal data, and personal accounts. Similar experiences were merged to maintain confidentiality of the nurses who shared their stories and work locations. Locations were hospitals, long-term care facilities, home health care settings, and in the academic setting. Nursing roles included staff nurses, educators, and administrators.

The American Nurse Association (ANA) code of ethics that requires nurses to create a culture of civility, kindness, and treating co-workers and others with dignity and respect. Let's see if you can see these behaviors in the following stories.

Scrutinization (Being Held to a Higher Standard)

I was told by my nurse manager that I would be under a microscope and that they were going to watch everything I did. But this was not told to my White peers. I felt depressed. My blood pressure went up. I also have role stress and I have all the strain. Don't minimize my feelings. Don't cut me off before I speak, stop saying the past is the past. We are in the 21st century and I'm still experiencing the same behaviors that other Black nurses from generations ago experienced.

Let's have some straight talk.

De-Legitimization of the Professional Role (Being De-valued)

Faculty of color experience invalidation of their sense of self, which jeopardizes their wellbeing. Nurses of color are channeled in low-status units where advancement is limited and there is a higher chance of injury.

As educators, we are seen as one with knowledge to impart to others. Unfortunately, this knowledge is not received by our peers or students. There are still questions like "Who are you? You are the teacher?" I must have my white coat on. It's like I must buck myself up with a lot of other things saying like who I am and what I am doing here. There is nobody that you can talk with who would respect you. You know the respect that you deserve in your professional role. It is almost like you are fighting for who you are. That is hard for me, and I see that every day. The recurring behaviors of being put in one's place are not new. It is a form of devaluing you as a professional.

Let me share a personal experience of being devalued

It was fall and I was looking out the window observing the beauty of the leaves that had changed colors. As I saw the leaves falling, I heard a knock on the door. I turned around to face the door, saw the student and welcomed her into the office.

The student started to complain about the grade she received on her assignment. I asked her to sit down so I could listen to her concerns and explain the reason she did not receive the full points.

As I was explaining the criteria that was missed, she let out a big sigh and stormed out of the office. I felt the air in the room shift from warm to cold.

I wondered what just happened. I felt disrespected as a professional and my heart started racing. That was my first teaching assignment and I have never heard of a student storming out of office hours in such a hurried manner without receiving full feedback.

What the student didn't realize is that I would have changed the grade if she could articulate the criteria she missed. I turned back to look out the window to see the leaves falling.

Two weeks had passed, and the student did not say one word to me. She responded to questions only in an abrupt way. Several hours later, it was time for the final examination. I was assisting the lead faculty with distribution of the examination. As I picked up the examinations, I noticed a stack of papers on the desk. On the top of the stack, I saw the student's name. The grade had been changed from a 65 out of 100 points to 95 points.

I was thinking, *how did this happen?* My colleague did not mention that she was going to regrade the paper. I felt confused and wondered, *what did I miss in the paper for a student to receive that many points?*

As the test came to close, the student walked up to the desk and turned her paper in. At that time, my colleague gave her the regraded paper. The student turned around, looked me in the eye and gave a smirk.

I couldn't believe it. The lead instructor changed the grade without my knowledge or approval.

The following is another example of being de-legitimized in the professional role.

They talked like I was the student or the small one in the room in a meeting. I felt like "What are you trying to do?" I felt attacked. The student felt like I was the instructor instead of the lead faculty. And I was thinking how all I did was give some feedback to the students. It was the [other] faculty member who did not call her [on it] so I had to call her [on it] so that she would learn from her mistake. It was not about the other faculty member it was about the student. But it really became about the other faculty member.

Personally, I was attacked, and I knew the reason it was done. It questioned my intelligence. I am sure other people would not tolerate that... I can't tell you how many times I have been told that I was grading the students too hard, yet when it came to grading Black students, I was not grading hard enough.

I was often asked to observe a Black student in the clinical setting. When asked for the reason why and what I was looking for, there was never a reason given. Black faculty are continually put in their place when providing input into course assignments and evaluations of White students. This constant behavior de-values and de-legitimizes the Black nurse in their profession role.

Take a few minutes, take a deep breath, and write down your feelings toward this story.

_____

_____

_____

_____

_____

_____

_____

Chapter 6

Horizontal Abuse

Horizontal abuse is described as a collection of negative behaviors and attitudes that do not view Black nurses in their professional achieved role—in their position of authority. An added component is feeling behaviorally abused by members of the same race and other oppressed minorities. The Black nurse is met with resistance and insubordination from the ancillary staff. For example, a Black nurse requested a wheelchair for her patient that was going to be transported off the floor for a scheduled test. The nursing assistant looked puzzled at this request and verbalized she was told not to do anything for this nurse. Now I thought, it is not about the nurse… it is about *the patient.*

Another example is when a Black nurse parked her car in a parking space designated for the employee of the month. Someone called security (the police) to report that a car was illegally parked in the space because they didn't know the car was in that space, even though it had the sticker. She had to be pulled out of her work environment and was met by the police to move her car. She was the employee of the month and she just happened to drive a different car to work.

When the nurses shared their stories, I observed a change in their facial expressions, their tone of voice became lower, and some teared up, as if the experience were yesterday. When I went back to review the recording, I could also see a change in their posture. Their posture went from a relaxed state before sharing their story to a tense state when recounting the experience.

I was told a story where a nurse was told to her face that she was obese and that is why she was given the fat patients. I was appalled.

And she went on to share how patient case assignments were given to her.

I noticed that I always was assigned heavy patients. I asked why I was getting all higher acuity patients, the response was: "Because you're obese and can relate to the patients. We thought you would be better suited to work with obese patients since you are obese."

A) nurse with less than ten years in the field shared how she felt abused in the work force as a registered nurse when she was told that her rate of speech was way too fast.

I was working hard, trying to do everything right. I dotted my i's and crossed my t's. I'm exhausted by the time I get home. All I can do is crawl into my bed knowing I have to start all over again tomorrow.

How do we educate our nursing students when experiencing this type of behavior?

A nurse educator responded:

I'm not educating students anymore.

I'm tired.

I'm not the nurse...

Chapter 7

Scrutinization

Scrutinization is described as being held to a higher standard. It was several months after I received my master's degree in community mental health, and I had filled out a couple of employment applications in the community and at some of the universities.

I was sitting at home on a Saturday doing my regular chores of dusting, washing dishes, and watching the kids playing in the backyard. The phone rang and I went to answer the phone using my at-home voice (Hello?) not my professional voice (Hello, my name is.... how can I help you) because it was Saturday. Who would be calling me of importance on the weekend?

I picked up the phone and said, "Hello?" The voice on the other end said, "May I speak with Ora Robinson? This is the secretary from X University and the lead faculty would like to speak with her. I was getting excited at that point at the prospect of being hired at a prestigious university. I was thinking *who would call you on a Saturday to tell you no?*

"We have your application here." The lead faculty got on the telephone, and she proceeded to drill me on my qualifications. She had my resume and asked me questions about my master's program and if I had any experience teaching.

My response was that I didn't have formal teaching experience with students at a college, but I have teaching experience based on my achieved role as an oncology nurse. This includes teaching patients, their family members, nursing students, and working as a preceptor for new graduates. That was the extent of my teaching experience. She went on to say that she was concerned that I didn't have "real" teaching experience with students.

At that time, I was thinking, *everybody knows that in nursing, if you're precepting students, you must know how to teach them and reinforce their learning objectives with consultation with the nursing faculty.*

She continued to drill me. and Abruptly, she verbalized that I would not be a good fit at the clinical site because they were very particular about who works with them.

At that point, I was getting really confused because clinical partners do not have a say on who gets hired. They do have a say on who they want at their site based on past experiences with the instructor or based on unprofessional behavior toward staff or nursing students. I knew the clinical site was in the suburbs where Blacks are not welcomed.

She went on to talk about this and that. I was thinking *you are wasting my time.* A little voice inside my head was saying, *you know, you're calling me on the weekend. I got excited at the thought that if someone calls on me on the weekend, it must be important.* I thanked her for the call. A couple of days later, I received a call again from that school on behalf of the Dean who wanted to inquire about my qualifications.

I got really perturbed again. I informed the dean that they have my transcripts and my resume, *what else did they need to know?*

She inquired about my master's degree project in the community with minority women. I elaborated in detail how I worked with a diverse population of women from different socioeconomic statuses, races, and ethnicities. I worked with women who represented cultural diversity and women from prison as well. I reiterated to her that although I lacked formal academic teaching experience with students in a university setting, I interacted with students in the role as the primary nurse of patients they were caring for and offering supervision in collaboration with their faculty when students are on the floor at various levels of their curriculum.

I was tired of the inquisition related to my qualifications. I calmly stated, "When I get the degrees to qualify, I don't have the experience. Who will give me the opportunity to have the experience?"

There was a pause, it felt like forever, but the pause was about a minute. The voice on the other end of the phone went on to say that she is aware of the American conflict with race. My ears perked up, she went on to say the lead faculty was reluctant to hire me.

I was tired of the stupid questions and continued inquisition of my qualifications from a reputable teaching hospital and university. I said "Look, send me the syllabus to review the learning objectives. If I can't implement at this level, I will be honest and tell you." She agreed and the phone call ended. I wondered if all candidates went through that degree of inquisition.

The syllabus arrived in the mail two days later. I reviewed the learning objectives and deemed I could implement these learning objectives. I was thinking, *I just finished a program, had a clinical experience, and I'm a practicing nurse in oncology/psychiatry.* I had extensive orientation in psychiatric nursing and mental health which was the teaching position being applied for.

I received a call from the director of nursing a couple of days later inviting me for an interview with her that Tuesday and I accepted. The meeting went well, and she verbalized an interest in wanting to hire me.

A second interview was scheduled. As I entered the interview room, I met eight White faces staring back at me. As I scanned the room, I could find no smiles and the room felt cold. I kept scanning and landed on a face that had a smile on it and the voice welcomed me. She was my co-worker from the oncology unit.

The other faces look stoic. I was dressed for success. I had on my suit, my low heel pumps, and minimal make-up. I took off any jewelry that would be intimidating.

Before I could sit down and put my portfolio on the desk, I was bombarded with questions about my master's clinical experience and why I wanted to be an adjunct faculty. What is my teaching philosophy?

It felt like a firing squad as those questions came out as rapid fire, giving me no time to formulate an adequate response. Thank God I worked in psychiatry where I am accustomed to rapid and disorganized speech patterns.

I know I could not say I never wanted to be an adjunct faculty. I couldn't say my mentor told me it was the next logical progression to demonstrate application of the content learned in my master's specialty of community mental health. But I heard those words come out of my mouth.

I indicated it was the next level of progressing since attaining my master's and I would be the first generation in my family to secure a teaching position at a prestigious university. I told them how I would like to pursue teaching at an academic level that goes beyond patient teaching and family teaching.

I shared my teaching philosophy; that every individual has the capacity to learn at their own level of understanding. It's up to the faculty to adapt their teaching strategies to meet the student at their level of understanding and to help the learner understand.

The next question was about my leadership style. I was glad I have read books on diverse leadership styles. My leadership style is multifaceted based on the many assessments taken over the years since the age of 16, working in corporate America. I am glad to say I have matured in my leadership style to be one that empowers others to share their gifts.

The discussion went something like this:

As a leader, my goal is to give opportunities to team members to self-discover their leadership capacity and give them opportunities to engage in leadership activities. For example, I put students in the role of a charge nurse and nurse supervisor at the foundation level. This translates into not being a micro manager and having confidence that they can do the job.

This philosophy is grounded in transformative leadership and empowerment of employees which allows for active participation in strategic planning. Based on my answers to the Multifactor Leadership Questionnaire, I was put in the category of transformative leadership. This leadership category is described as having the ability to be proactive and optimize individuals, groups, organizational development, and innovation.

The Maxwell Leadership Assessment positioned me into the category of people development. People's development is described as one who embraces the development of others. My experiential and academic knowledge is used to reproduce those skills in others. These are consistent with my personal mission to inspire, motivate, and educate one nurse or individual at a time to achieve their goal. This is demonstrated in mentoring students and coaching nurses in transition at various stages of their career ladder.

Their faces were still emotionless. I was thinking, *no one prepared me for an interview like this.*

Another committee member asked a question about childcare. *Whose business is it anyway? Isn't this question illegal?*

My response was, "If I accept a position, I can be at the organization at the designated time frame. (heck I've done it for ten years)."

At that point, I thought, *I don't need this job. I have a full-time job. I'm happy with helping people transition at the end of life.* Having 22 years at a teaching hospital and four-week vacations, I had no desire to leave. The desire was to maximize my master's degree and go to the next step.

A familiar voice, my colleague, chimed in and verbalized to the rest of the committee that I had excellent work ethics, was a pleasure to work with, and would be a good addition to the staff. To this day, I believe if it weren't for my colleague, I would not have gotten that opportunity.

Chapter 8

The Orientation:
Baptism by Fire

U pon arriving at the school, I was excited as I walked down the halls of wisdom. I was scheduled to meet the team lead for orientation. I was in a positive mood because I was happy to be in the halls of higher education. I recall watching the television show, Dobie Gillis during the 60s which opened with the Thinking Man. The TV series, A Different World, during the late 80'S, showed Blacks engaged in college and campus life. I thought to myself, I have arrived.

As I walked into the office, there was a chill in the air as I was directed to sit on the chair. Professor X walked over to me and said a dry "Good morning," gave me a packet, and indicated she would speak with me after the lecture. There was no information on the location of the break room or where I could find nourishment or coffee.

In the meantime, I sat on the chair for two hours. I thought, *okay, I'm getting paid for sitting.* There was no orientation to her expectations or what philosophy the nursing program was following. She gave me the student roster, the name of the clinical site, and the contact person.

There was no orientation on to how to manage the clinical environment and the expectations of the facility. In addition, there was no discussion on how to manage the students in the clinical environment. I thought to myself, *this lady wants me to fail.*

As I was leaving her office, she told me to take a seat and another professor will be coming from the educational department to orient me on the principles of education. As I sat on the chair, I smelled cologne—a woodsy smell. I looked up to see a man standing and asking if I was Ora.

He extended his hand for a shake and introduced himself as my mentor for the teaching component. I received a handshake. I was pleasantly surprised as the approach was totally different from the person earlier. He walked me over to his office and proceeded to orient me regarding the expectations of the role of an educator. I thought I would have to draw on my experience as a student and the teaching strategies used by a few good teachers to implement the role of the clinical faculty.

He took the time to discuss the academic theories being used in higher education, gave me a binder on adult learning theories, and the teachers' manual on dimensions of learning which included the five types of thinking in dimensions listed below:

1. Positive attitudes and perceptions about learning.

2. Thinking involved in acquiring and integrating knowledge.

3. Thinking involved in extending and refining knowledge.

4. Thinking involved in using knowledge meaningfully.

5. Productive habits of the mind.

The manual gave planning for these dimensions and case studies for application.

The Skillful Teacher was another book given by the professor. He said this book is golden as it discusses what you did not learn in school. The book reviewed the range of skills needed in the classroom and provided feedback on how to thrive in an unpredictable environment. The author referred to the book as a manual of survival.

My mentor and I met at scheduled times to discuss any questions on the readings. In addition, he asked about my teaching experiences in the clinical environment with student management. He generously offered insights and practical strategies that can be easily integrated.

He shared his insights on how to manage student outbursts in an unpredictable diverse environment. This laid the foundation for my teaching instructional methodology. For example, I incorporate Socratic questioning to facilitate student engagement, role play patient scenarios, and have low-fidelity simulations.

Galatians 6:9

"And let us not be weary in well doing for in due season we shall reap; if we faint not."

Chapter 9

White Privilege, In Our Words

Psalm 30: 13,4

"For I have heard the slander of many; fear was on every side; while they took counsel together against me; they devised to

take away my life. But I trusted the Lord; deliver me from the hand of my enemies and from those that persecute me."

I bought into the promise of the American dream. If you work hard, stay out of trouble, stay off the welfare, follow the rules, get educated, marry, and have a house with the white picket fence, you can achieve any of your goals which are available opportunities for every citizen. I did not know the pursuit of the American dream and the pursuit of happiness was not for Black Americans. Well, I followed the rules and got nothing but misery, frustration, and heartache in return.

There were times when I contemplated the consequences of not following the rules. I immediately envisioned hell and prison. I reflected on those who came before me, those who fought the good fight of faith so I could be included in the American dream. I ran the race and endured the pain and frustration without losing my sanity and wearing a yellow jumpsuit.

At times, it would have been easier to quit, but I always reminded myself that those before me did not quit so that I could have this opportunity. The women in my family did not quit. I have endured the pain, ran the race, and maintained my sanity, psychological wellbeing, and physical health through it all. I did not have a nervous breakdown, and I did not have a life-threatening illness due to the pain.

My Humble Beginnings of Being Invisible

You may be wondering, *why is the writer going back to her childhood?* Not until I embarked on this book project, did I realize that being invisible was put into my subconsciousness by a teacher at an early age. Therefore, I want to share this story as a testament of how I was made to feel invisible.

Being invisible started for me while in elementary school when I was put in speech class because I could not pronounce the "sh" and "ch" sounds. At that tender age, I was told I should not work in any job that requires speaking. Being only around eight or nine years old, I did not have a clue what she was talking about. I had no reference point concerning race as my friends were of diverse backgrounds—Native American, White, and Hispanic. I did not know enough to tell my mother who would certainly have come down to the school and told that teacher a thing or two.

Another instructor in elementary school refused to let me take piano classes because I did not have a piano at home. My mother explained to her that I had access to three pianos. There was a piano at church, at my mother's girlfriend house, and at the parents of my girlfriend's house who have offered their piano for practice. The instructor did not change her mind and I couldn't take piano lessons.

You may wonder, *how does this discussion fit with the theme of the invisible Black nurse?*

First, this is my story. Second, it shows how at an early age, I was perceived as less than—less competent, and those opinions of us from others unconsciously were etched in my young mind. To this day, it bothers me that one person hindered me from trying to play the piano which meant I could have learned how to read and write musical notes. These stories demonstrate persistence and perseverance as I went into nursing school and worked as a registered nurse. I didn't succumb to the pressure, and I did not quit.

This message of not being good enough extended into high school when the counselor told me not to pursue any occupation in the medical field based on my test scores. Therefore, I did not take chemistry in high school, but I completed the basic science course. The counselor left me with the words: "You could not become anything in medicine or health because of your lack of science background."

Upon graduating high school at 17 years old, I received a scholarship to a community college. The high school counselor directed me to study secretarial science. I thought, I already have the course work in secretarial science by having completed three years of office education with on-the-job training. I attained the highest shorthand speed of 120 and had a typing speed of 80.

He then said, he did me a favor by giving me the scholarship instead of giving it to the White female or male student. Humph, not sure how to take that one. The White privilege in this is believing he had the right to dictate my future. Why should I continue the same course of study when I have attained competency?

I now understand what our office education instructor meant when she said the Negro was at a disadvantage at the starting gate. She said we were being taught shorthand at 80 wpm compared to the private and more influential public schools which were teaching students' shorthand at 80 wpm. Because of this injustice, she was defiant and taught her negro students shorthand at 120 wpm. Typing was taught at influential schools at 70 wpm, and we were taught at 80 wpm. This is my first awareness of disparities in education and systemic racism. She left us with the message that we can achieve if given a level playing field.

The office education teacher explained to us that by teaching us at higher speeds in the public education system, we would be at the same level of speed as the suburban school system. This would give us the same advantage based on our typing and shorthand speed to be equally competitive based on our skills.

When I got to community college, I went ahead and signed up for advanced stenography to find they were teaching below the level I was taught in high school. Thank God for Ms. Z. who taught us at the same level of the suburban schools. When I took those classes at the community college, the instructor asked me why I was in the class as I had already met competencies.

I signed up for the combined anatomy and physiology course. I was excited to learn about the human body. My excitement quickly diminished as the instructor would never call on me when I would raise my hand. Over and over this occurred. I then looked around the room and notice another Black student who also was not called on when she would raise her hand. It became apparent that this was another situation of feeling invisible.

I had no idea of the events to come next. I was walking in my neighborhood to go to my ophthalmologist. Upon entering the lobby of the medical office building, I saw one of the students from the anatomy and physiology class come out from another office. Our eyes met and I said hi. She responded hi and asked what office was I working out of? I responded by saying I was not working out of the office, I was coming in for my eye appointment. She looked puzzled. I then said, how did you find this job? She went on to say that the faculty shared this job opportunity with several students after class. At that point, I was dumbfounded.

You may wonder, why would I be astonished? Because I lived in walking distance from the medical office building, as well as the other Black student and we were not told of this opportunity. The student who secured the position lived in the suburbs. Are you scratching your head yet?

After fifteen years, I returned to college, completed my baccalaureate degree, and became a clinical nurse specialist in Oncology and Psychiatric nursing. Upon completion of my doctorate in Human Services, I became an assistant professor in higher education. I have experienced horizontal abuse as a clinical nurse specialist and as an academician. I am intimately familiar with my role being marginalized, delegitimized, and being held to a higher standard than my peers.

What was most disturbing was to know that my White peers did not want me to instruct White students or give them negative feedback. Papers were changed, lectures were retaught behind my back, and students were coerced into writing negative student evaluations. Let's look at what happened while I was in nursing school.

Chapter 10

Delegitimization of the Professional Role

Proverbs 23:9

"Do not speak in the hearing of a fool, for he will despise the wisdom of your words."

This chapter discusses different encounters that reflect not being valued in your achieved role. Being devalued is defined as the delegitimization of the professional role. The roles include that of a nursing student and working as a staff nurse. The term "encounter" will be used to depict such examples.

First Encounter

Fifteen years have passed since that awful experience at the community college when I arrived at the college of nursing to further my education. I was summoned to the assistant dean's office. I got on the elevator to the seventh floor. I was wondering, *what could she possibly want?* I was wondering if all new students were usually called to her office for a welcome by leadership.

As I walked into her office, her eyes met mine and she told me (not asked) to take a seat. Her face was in the "resting bitch mode" and there was no smile on her face. She looked me directly in the eyes. She went on to say I would not be receiving a baccalaureate degree from this school.

My eyes stayed locked on hers as I processed what I just heard. She went on to verbalize that I needed to go back and study being a medical record librarian because I will not be receiving a nursing degree from this school. At that point, I was baffled.

I was admitted to nursing school, but before I could respond, she dismissed me from her office. She stood up from her chair and looked down at me. This is another example of White privilege, standing over me. I stood up, thanked her for the visit, and left.

My feet took me right to the seventh-floor bathroom. As I looked in the mirror, tears started to flow down my cheeks. What just happened? My tears were of anger, frustration, and bewilderment. I was accepted into the program, I had classes, *what was she talking about?!* The terms "institutional racism and systemic racism" entered my mind. I have heard of these terms, but never experienced it.

Being in my thirties, I had common sense and knew not to play into her hand. My daddy taught me poker—holding a poker face, and how to call a bluff. I decided to make an appointment to see the dean. In addition, I sought counsel from my obstetrician, a renowned Black physician in the community who had a wealth of knowledge on how to navigate institutional racism. He and his wife sat on hospital boards. Dr. X would share stories of his experiences during a time when they were relegated to bypass the White hospitals and work at the Black hospitals. He would always say, "This will pass." To this day, he intervened in some way as I never had an encounter with that woman again in a professional capacity.

That was my first personal experience with institutional or systemic racism. I read about those in research. I realized she was a gatekeeper of knowledge. Blacks not allowed.

In all my frustration, I didn't realize I should have reported it to the federal organization that gives out federal grants based on diversity. What angered me most was the assistant dean was the representative for diversity inclusion and attended most diversity events. In her position on behalf of the school, she received federal funding while encouraging Black students to withdraw from the nursing program and go to a community college—such a hypocrite.

Take a pause and reflect. Take a few minutes to jot down some of your reactions to this story. What are you thinking? What are you feeling? What lessons were learned?

_____

_____

_____

_____

Lessons learned:

_____

_____

_____

Second Encounter:

After graduating from nursing school, I returned to work as a registered nurse at the hospital where I worked as a medical transcriber. The hospital had a scholarship for minority employees. The purpose was to develop their employees from within to become registered nurses. The scholarship paid for all expenses. The beauty of the scholarship was that your seniority kept accruing and you received your paycheck.

After I graduated, I did not pass the boards on the first, second, or the third attempt. In the meantime, I worked as a nursing assistant. I will not discuss the treatment I received at that level, but it made me more empathetic to the role of the nursing assistant and my first encounter with nurses eating their young. This means nurses are not supportive of each other.

Even though I was a graduate nurse, some nurses were indifferent and gave me jobs like cleaning up the break table or the computer screens and giving me a list of activities to do for each hour of the shift. I remember taking that paper, balling it up and throwing into the trash can. The shift was the third shift.

When I passed the boards, I was excited. I put aside my anxiety and got the job done. The common practice was to be put into a position as a registered nurse. The transition was less than a week and orientation to the role started the next week.

To my surprise, I was told I had to take a remediation course. The remediation course was for nurses who have been out of the field for five or more years.

When my peers found out I received a full scholarship that included accrual of seniority, a group of nurses tried to go down to the city office and have the regulation removed so I would have to work third shift and lose all seniority. Yes, I am not making this up as I am not this creative.

Third Encounter:

My third encounter was when a nurse on third shift informed the nursing supervisor (not the charge nurse) that I incorrectly documented the physical assessment on a patient. I was still on orientation being precepted by another RN. The nurse who reported me to the nursing supervisor was all smiles when she saw me. As I entered the office, I was thinking, here we go again, *when does it stop?*

The nursing supervisor began to bombard me with questions such as, why I did not document the findings under the nursing notes, saying: "Do you know you could lose your license? This is unacceptable, let me see your assignment sheet and care plan."

The method of charting was by exception. This is a method where there is a check box and if there is an abnormal finding, you check the box and then write a note on the nursing note page.

I handed the supervisor my assignment sheet and care plans. I informed her that the patient in question was not on my case load. As she looked closely at the signature and the initials, she realized it was the preceptor who had this patient. She offered an apology. I inquired about the source of this information and of course she could not disclose the source.

Fourth Encounter:

I was assigned three patients with HIV and one with AIDs along with an oncology patient. As I was sitting in the report room receiving my assignment, I asked if it was policy that we mixed infectious patients with an immunocompromised patient. I was wondering why the infectious patients were not distributed among the nurses.

There were no changes, therefore I cared for the immunocompromised patient first. If you are wondering, yes, I followed up with the nursing supervisor and she indicated it was okay, there was no problem with the assignment. This happened during a time when HIV/AIDs were new.

I embraced the challenge and was able to become an expert in the progression as each patient was at a different level. It was humbling to hear their stories of how they were infected. After these stories, any bias I had toward this population was removed.

One of the patients died during my shift. The family came out and thanked me for caring for their loved one despite his condition and combative behavior. The behavior was due to the infection ravishing his brain. The family mentioned I was the first nurse to touch their loved one and offer them comfort. Tears swelled up in my eyes. I could only respond with a thank you. The patient was Black, and I will never know if the lack of touch was related to his diagnosis or his being Black. I am left thinking we can't even die in peace.

I was fed up with uncaring nursing behaviors and channeled that negative energy into pursuing a master's in community mental health. Something happened on the way to attaining my master's. I met another gatekeeper in my research class, Measurement in Nursing Research." One of the authors of the textbook we were to read was Dr. Ora L. Strickland. I was excited to see another Ora who had achieved what I was trying to. Through her writings, she was a silent mentor without her knowing.

At any rate, my instructor asked the class their reasons for taking this class. When it was my turn, I told them how my advisor gave approval to take this course as it would be beneficial to understand the research process, as I aspired to obtain my doctorate degree.

The look on the professor's face was quite frightening. I thought she was having an aneurysm as her lips started to quiver. If her looks could kill, I would be dead.

She then blurted out in front of the students that I didn't belong here. I thought, *yes, I belong, I got approval. Okay, you can pick up your jaw from the floor* .

We had a group assignment due which was turned in that day. I worked with two other students in the class. The next week, she returned every student's assignment except mine. I wondered where my assignment was. I turned it in. The group members received an A.

As we left for a break, she asked me to stay after class, she wanted to speak with me. When the students had left, she blurted out, "You will not be getting the grades you need to have for it to count to your graduate degree."

I quickly read between the lines and dug real deep to not let tears flow and my emotions show on my face, so I maintained my poker face. My voice softly asked what would she suggest. I already knew the answer, but I had to stay focused on my goal.

Her response was to take the course as an audit which would not count toward my degree requirements. I told her I would think about it and get back to her. Her deadline was at 8:00 p.m. and it was already 7:30 p.m. I quickly called my advisor and updated her on the situation. She acknowledged it was wrong and said I had to make a choice to fight this battle or win the war.

We are duty bound with the ethical principles of autonomy (self-determination), non-maleficence (avoid causing harm), beneficence (benefit the patient), justice (act fairly), and fidelity (keeping promise to use one's competence to benefit those in our care).

In addition, we are charged with the professional values of altruism (concern for the well-being of others which includes your peers), autonomy, human dignity (respect and valuing patient's and colleagues), integrity (acting within the code of ethics), and social justice (supporting non-discrimination in patient care delivery).

Take this time to reflect. Have you been adhering to the code of ethics and professional standards of nursing while interacting with your peers from diverse socioeconomic, racial, ethnicity, cultural, gender, age, and those from the LGBT community?

Remember, love conquers all.

_____

_____

_____

_____

Lessons learned:

_____

_____

_____

_____

_____

_____

_____

Chapter 11

Holding Onto
my Sanity

Romans 8:28

*"And we know that God causes all things to work
together for good to those who love God, to those who
are called according to His purposes."*

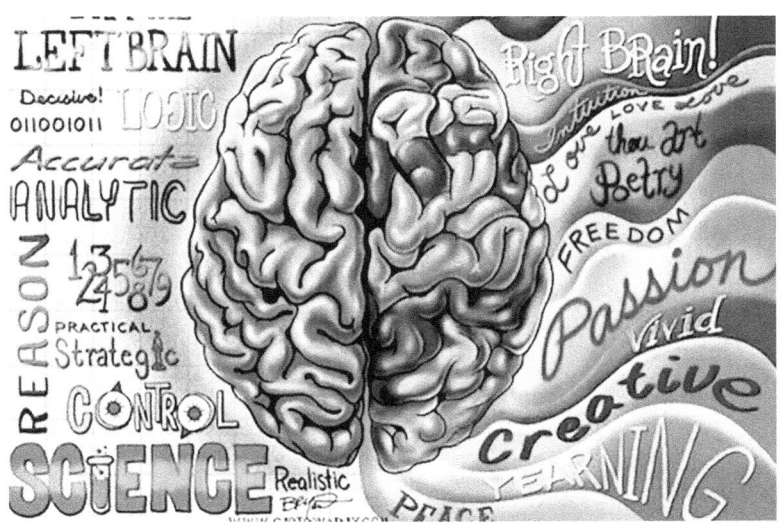

I am trying to hold onto my intellectual capacity while working with individuals whose intellectual capacity is limited. Don't be mad at me. You made me smarter than I had to be. Say what? Yes, all those barriers you placed in front of me with the intent to stop me. *Remember now?*

Remember, when you gave me an assignment in medical surgical nursing with a patient with respiratory problems and we were studying the GI system?

I arrived at the floor to find my patient had COPD and asthma and we had not covered that material in lecture. *Now, do you remember?* But I pushed through because I know to study beyond what we are learning for times such as this. I flipped that into a challenge.

Remember, you told me to present a care plan in 30 minutes for the care of a patient with respiratory problems? And I did. I'm not going to tell you how I did it. You meant to hold me back but here I stand.

God turned it around for good.

Genesis 50:20

"But as for you, ye thought evil against me; but God meant it unto good, to bring to pass, as it is this day, to save much people alive."

I turned it into a challenge and got through the day.

Take a moment to reflect on your mental health.

_____

_____

_____

_____

I am trying to maintain my mental health while working with some individuals whose mental health is void of compassion, empathy, or love. A nurse who loves their fellow man, would not put a patient at risk, to cause potential harm to the patient to blame another nurse and potentially get the nurse fired or lose their license. Really!!!

Even if you have bias and unconscious bias, you should follow the ethical principles of beneficence (acting with kindness and sympathy to benefit others) and maleficence (to cause no harm). I am trying to hold onto my peace, my passion, my creativity, and love for my fellow nurses.

Do you remember what you did? Take a few moments and reflect on your near-miss experiences with this type of behavior.

_____

_____

_____

_____

Chapter 12

I Am Not the Help

T his chapter describes the experiences of being devalued in the professional achieved role of the nurse. The first impression is based on their race (ascribed). Black nurses are constantly confronted with being assumed to be the housekeeper or the certified nursing assistant, and not as a professional nurse. Their credentials are constantly questioned as they strive to care for those entrusted to their care.

Narrative A: Balancing Racial Incivility

Figure 1. Balancing acts of horizontal abuse in the form of racial incivility.

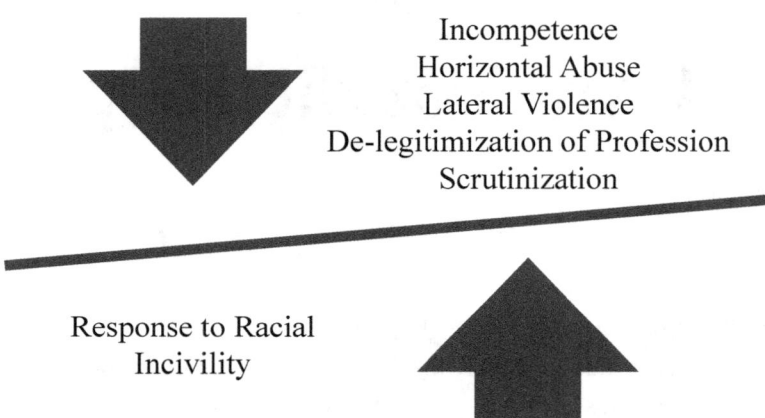

Incompetence
Horizontal Abuse
Lateral Violence
De-legitimization of Profession
Scrutinization

Response to Racial
Incivility

The above graphic depicts the balancing act Black nurses must navigate through in their professional achieved role as an RN. The graphic depicts that first impression experienced by Black nurses in the trenches. They were looked at in terms of our race which led to feelings of frustration and sadness for the patient. We look past their behavior and continue to provide quality and compassionate care. Again, this is not a battle to fight. In our minds, we have moved past our racial category. We have moved into our professional role. We went to school, we received the credentials of an RN, and yet we must experience an inquisition with a series of questions such as:

▷ are we the housekeeper?

▷ are we the CNA?

▷ are you sure you can do this?

> ▷ I want a White nurse.

> ▷ are you an LVN?

> ▷ what school did you attend, was it accredited?

We're constantly having to explain our role.

> ▷ Yes, I am a registered nurse. Then my achieved role.

> ▷ Yes, I graduated from an accredited college.

> ▷ Yes, I passed the state boards.

The first and second impression leads to role stress and strain. Therefore, I am conflicted between who I am: a registered nurse who happens to be Black, or a Black nurse who is a registered nurse? The result, racial incivility for Black nurses because of negative racial perspectives from patients and acts of racial oppression from our nurse colleagues.

It gets better… based on the school we graduated from, we must hear negative things about the school which implies we are "less than" by association.

The recurring findings emerge as feeling invisible with physical and psychological effects. One nurse in her 70's shares an experience she had over fifty years ago.

I received my doctorate and was returning to my office. In the distance, I could see the banner of congratulations and other accolades. As I got closer to my office, I saw some of my colleagues tearing down the banners. My eyes swelled up with tears as I approached my office. Anger filled my belly.

As she shared her story, her eyes filled up with tears and her voice cracked. You could hear the pain in her voice as if it happened yesterday, yet it was over fifty years ago.

Even though you have a white lab coat on with RN in big print, we are still asked who we are. We expect that from patients, but not from our peers.

We are constantly questioned about our credentials. It sounds like this: What school did you graduate from? They then proceed to say disparaging things about the school. It looks like this... your director grabbing your name badge and saying, "Just because you have these initials doesn't mean you can do what it says."

My response is no response as I reflect on their inability to complete their comprehensives to even start the doctoral process at the Ph.D. level. In addition, I reflect on the scriptural verse that implies not to respond to fools who lack wisdom.

This section is for all nurses who have felt devalued and abused based on a peer trying to hold you down based on any of the protected isms.

▷ I am not the housekeeper.

One nurse verbalized the following:

I entered the patient's room with my lab coat on and big RN initials on my name badge. The patient looked at me and asked for her nurse. I informed her that I was her nurse and she asked if I was the housekeeper.

Another participant shared an experience where her self-esteem was shattered. The following are her words:

I was given case load of obese clients. I asked why was I getting this number of obese clients? The response I got floored me. The response was that because I was obese, I could better manage the clients.

Delegitimization of the Professional Role

"They talk to me as if I am the ancillary staff and not their peer." "They don't ask me, they tell me." "They specifically tell me when I will have lunch." "My time here is closely monitored compared to my peers."

Other nurses stated:

"Why are you bothering me? I'm on break." This is amidst a pandemic when all nurses are stressed to the max and one Black nurse can't have fifteen minutes of solitude without being questioned before returning to the war zone.

Even during the time of the pandemic, stories still emerge as being treated differently and encouraged to be on the front line. Here's one nurse's story: She works in the ICU and has been a nurse for over 25 years. She has experienced constant interruptions while taking a break.

She shared another experience where her assessment findings were questioned. The patient had developed a temperature and was exhibiting the basic signs of COVID. She requested the patient to be transferred to the COVID unit. This request was not acted upon until later in the evening when the algorithm indicated the patient had COVID.

Again, invisibility set in while she pondered why her assessment was not acted upon. Are we still invisible during a pandemic? The answer is yes, and no. Fellow nurses are willing to put us on the front line of COVID but not listen to our assessments. The pendulum continues to swing away from caring and we need to get back to the center of caring for each other. Or was there ever a time that we cared for each other?

The following stories have not been changed from their voice for the reader to get a sense of what the Black nurse is experiencing in their own words. The Black nurse was attending a meeting and contemplating bringing up an issue around diversity. Let's look at what she said.

I remember sitting in a [meeting room] debating whether I was even going to bring it up because I was playing out what was going to happen in my head. And it was almost like a joke. And almost like a game for me... my image was throwing a bone and dogs devouring it, which is what happened.

I threw the bone out. I said, "What about diversity?" And immediately "Well, why are you bringing that up? What are you talking about? Are people complaining? What examples do you have? Can we operationalize diversity? I just sat back and said nothing more than that. And everyone was going on about this issue. And eventually it got quiet, and they were like—I guess I wasn't talking anymore—and someone said "Well [X], could you elaborate?" And I said, "No, forget it." I withdrew. I withdrew the point.

This behavior is familiar to me as I reflect on many meetings where I would offer a different perspective or bring up the need to consider cultural diversity and would be shut down. It was easy for me to default back to my shyness and staying in my place. You are then labeled "not a team player" by not participating in the discussion.

Chapter 13

Nurses Eating Their Black Young

“ “**N**urses eating their young” is a phenomenon in nursing who are not welcoming to new or younger nurses coming into the profession. These behaviors have ranged from incivility, horizontal and lateral abuse, bullying, and racial bullying. These behaviors have negative effects on the new nurses and potentially on the patients they care for. Black nurses experience this behavior on a higher degree and more frequently than other minority groups and their White peers. This behavior also is encountered by some other Black nurses. Here are some examples.

Horizontal Abuse

As a new graduate nurse in the bone marrow unit, I asked a Black nurse a question, and her response surprised me as it was abrupt. She looked me right in the eyes without a smile and stated, “No one helped me so you will have to figure it out.” Wow! I thought, she would be more supportive as we were the only Black nurses in the unit, and two of five in the entire nursing profession at the hospital. My first encounter of being “eaten by your peer” was from a fellow Black nurse. This encounter introduced me to the phenomenon of nurses eating their young. This began my journey of many more experiences of being eaten by my peers and not feeling visible in my role as a professional registered nurse.

De-legitimization of the Professional Role

Another experience was with a physician who refused to acknowledge me as his patient's nurse. He continued to talk with the White nurse about the patient. I was sitting at the nurses' station reviewing charts and documenting in the nursing notes. I saw the physician lean across the counter and asked who was caring for this patient. I got up from my chair, walked over to the counter, and identified myself as the nurse caring for his patient. He turned his head and started speaking to a nurse he was friendly with. He began to speak about his patient. Again, I Interrupted and introduced myself as the nurse. Again, he did not look at me and proceeded to give verbal orders to the White nurse. I walked away but stayed close enough to listen. The other nurse did not at any time, stop the physician and redirect him to me. *The White nurse was refusing to acknowledge my visibility as a nurse.* She listened to the order, but never recorded it in the chart. The physician turned around and walked away.

I could feel the coldness in the air as she approached me. She leaned over my shoulder and began to repeat the order the physician gave to her. I looked up from my chair and told her, "No, I'm not taking a verbal physician's order from you." Her facial features went into the resting bitch mode. She repeated the order again (I was thinking, *what doesn't she understand and is she trying to get me fired before I even started my career?*) and she said it again. Looking at her, directly into her baby blue eyes, I told her she received the order, and she is responsible for documenting the order in the chart. I heard a deep sigh as she stormed off.

I got up from the chair, went over to the chart carrousel, and to my surprise she did not document the verbal order in the chart.

About 10 minutes later, I could hear the wheels of the transportation gurney. The transporter asked to speak to the nurse assigned to the patient. I got up from the chair and introduced myself as the nurse. The transporter verbalized that the rehabilitation unit would not receive the patient due to the PICC line being still inserted.

The physician was yelling at the top of his voice, "Who's caring for my patient?" For some reason, I decided not to be scared or anxious because of his behavior. I identified myself as the assigned nurse. He proceeded to yell at me in front of the nurses' station and all eyes were on me. I stayed calm and allowed him to finish. I walked over to the carousel, pulled out the patient's chart, placed it on the counter, and showed him there was no written order to remove the PICC line. I told him I did not receive a verbal order but was aware that he gave a verbal order to the unassigned nurse.

In the meantime, the house supervisor came up and wanted to know what was going on. The physician pointed at me and said, "That nurse did not carry out my verbal order." At that point, I thought, is he color blind? Did he not remember who he gave the order to?

The house supervisor asked the physician to identify the nurse he gave the verbal order to. He looked puzzled and pointed to the other nurse standing by the carousel. The supervisor summoned the nurse over. I could see the nurse's face changing to shades of pink. The supervisor asked her if she verbally received the verbal order. When her mouth opened, her tone changed from being aggressive with me to using a soft tone with the supervisor. She replied, "Yes but I communicated it to Ora."

At that point, the supervisor indicated to the physician that the order was not communicated to the correct nurse and the order was not written in the chart. Therefore, there was no order to be carried out. The house supervisor gave him the chart to write the order. She went on to reprimand him for yelling at her nurses in front of the nursing station. She went on to say it was the fault of the nurse who did not document the order in the chart. She went on to say that our protocol is that nurses do not receive a verbal order from another nurse. The nurse who receives the order is responsible for recording it in the chart.

You may be wondering, *why didn't I just write down the order since I heard it anyway?* The order was not given directly to me, and the physician did not acknowledge me as the nurse. I reflected on the ethical principle of nonmaleficence (do not harm, seek not to do harm). Being transported with the PICC line did not cause harm. The IV team was notified and the PICC line was removed, and the patient was re-transported to the rehabilitation unit within 30 minutes.

Take some time to reflect on these two stories. Reflect on how the stories make you feel. What would you have done differently in this kind of situation? Did you experience any physical, emotional, or psychological responses when faced with similar situations? Take a few minutes and use the lines below to respond to the questions.

How did the story make you feel?

Did you experience any physical responses? If yes, write them down.

_____

_____

_____

_____

Did you experience any emotional responses? If yes, write them down.

_____

_____

_____

_____

Did you experience any psychological responses? If yes, write them down.

_____

_____

_____

_____

Now that you've had an opportunity to read and reflect on the stories of being invisible, let's look at the health consequences that Black nurses experience because of horizontal abuse, scrutinization, and de-legitimization of the professional role.

HEALTH EFFECTS
OF RACIAL BULLYING

Chapter 14

Health Consequences
of Racial Bullying

This section describes the experiences that led to
adverse health consequences

3 John 1:2

*Beloved, I pray that all may go well with you and that
you may be in good health, as it goes well with your
soul.*

This chapter gives you a glimpse of the physical health consequences experienced by Black nurses when encountering acts of racism. The difficulty of writing this chapter made its way to the surface of my emotions as I sat down to write it. I will draw on research findings that looked at physical health and psychological health consequences after being exposed to acts of racism and share my experiences with physical health consequences.

Nurses who participated in a research study on Characteristics of Racism and health consequences (Robinson, 2014) reported increased symptoms of stress, increased physical complaints, and increased psychological complaints.

For example, Black nurses experience increased stress and increased activation of the sympathetic responses, which led to increased physical complaints as well as increased psychological complaints from the professional.

Blood pressure ranged from 140/100 to 180/200. There was no evidence of cardiac disease or heart attack, but the etiology was extreme stress. Additional symptoms included abdominal pain due to ulcers, which correlates with the health disparities in this population in general as it relates to race (Robinson, 2014, p. 133).

These experiences have led and still lead to adverse health effects experienced by Black nurses. Patient care did not suffer, although there was some change in the motivation to deliver quality patient care. The participants were eager to share their stories in hopes to eradicate this type of behavior among those in the nursing profession. Look at Figure 2 depicting the sequence of racial bullying.

Figure 2: Emerging graphic depiction of racial bullying

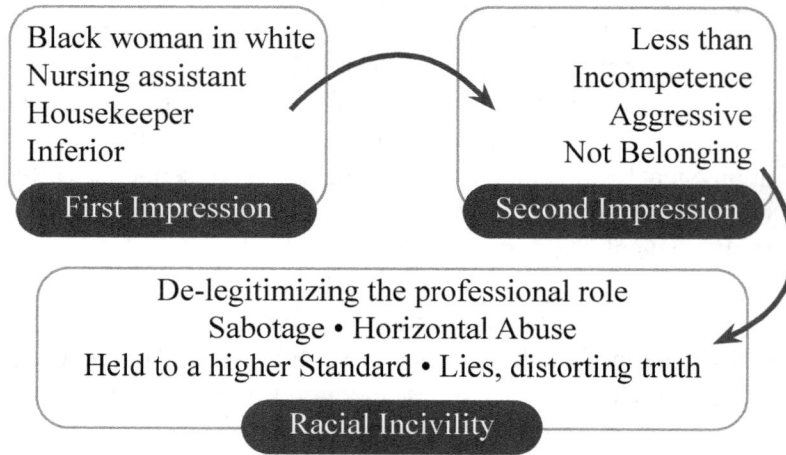

Physical Effects of Racial Bullying

My Personal Journey

Once I got into higher education it really took a turn. My hypertension went extremely high. My blood pressure ranged as high as 200/110 which is stroke level. I had to be transported from my place of employment to the emergency room after experiencing exposure to racism or racist acts from students.

Those who know me would describe me as passive and quiet, one who doesn't like to make trouble. Therefore, when I experienced events that I perceived as racism, I had to put myself on pause to monitor how to best respond. You may wonder, why pause? Well from my experience, when I responded, I would be accused of being defensive or being the angry Black woman.

What would I say? I can't say anything to make it worse. I thought, *I can't say anything to get fired. I can't say anything in front of students because I'm supposed to be a role model. Eyes on me, all 60 eyes on me.*

How do I respond? For example, I was interacting with a student, and we were laughing. I heard this voice in the background yelling out, "You are not professional, and you call yourself a professional, and you want us to be a professional."

I thought, *where is this coming from?* I turned to look, and I saw a student in scrubs pointing her finger at me. I thought, *oh my goodness. Oh, okay. How do I respond?* I was on the other side of the room. The class was on break during that time. You could hear a pin drop, all eyes on me.

101

Thankfully, I was able to diffuse the situation. As I was lecturing, she went the extra mile and asked why I was teaching that content? Why do they need to know what I was teaching when it wasn't on the syllabus, yada, yada.

At that point, I was in awe as I had never experienced an outburst like that in 25 years of teaching on my worst day. I tried to explain to her why she needed to know the material as it was a precursor for the additional content.

As I looked out into the classroom, I could see the heads nodding in agreement. Therefore, I asked, "How many other students do not want to hear this information?" All hands went up.

I said to myself, *okay, now I'm the teacher. These people are trying to be nurses, and yet they are telling me what they do not want to hear.* In the meantime, my blood pressure was boiling and boiling. I could feel my shoulders getting tight as I tried to explain again. I decided to bypass the material because sometimes, you must allow people to have their way and live through the consequences.

Therefore, I skipped that little section, and I went on to the next section that required an in-depth discussion. Then, suddenly, I heard voices saying, "Wait, wait, wait, we don't understand what you're saying." I calmly said, "Well, if you allowed me to have the prior discussion—the precursory discussion—we would not be in this situation.

At that point, I felt like packing my bags and calling it a day. *They can read the text and take the test. "You know what guys it's time for a break, okay?"*

Upon return from break, I thought about how I was going to handle this. I felt myself getting nervous on the inside because I have never experienced something like this before. I was in a situation where I could not hold the students accountable for their actions. Remember, the students are customers, and they are right.

The next day, I showed up to the same course but a different section. As I was speaking and interacting with the students— having fun, I heard a voice from the back ask, "Dr. Robinson, are you okay?"

I thought, *yes, I'm okay*. And then I felt a twinge in my chest. My chest was tightening up. And the voice asked again, "Dr. Robinson, are you okay?" I looked at the person and said, "No, I'm not okay. Can you go to the office and have them call 911 for me, please?"

It felt like an elephant was on my chest. Paramedics came and my blood pressure was 180/120. They transported me to the hospital. Luckily, I didn't have a heart attack or cardiac disease.

As I lay hooked up to different tubes and oxygen, I thought, *I do not have cardiac disease that has been ruled out historically as stress related.* I know from being a psychiatric nurse and a Christian when students go off on you, it is not about you. They have some underlying problem they are dealing with. They lash out at those they think may not respond kindly.

Here is an interesting point I didn't discuss earlier. Upon arrival in the emergency room, I had to wait on the gurney. I heard a voice say, "Dr. Robinson, why are you here?" (HIPAA violation), I looked up and who did I see? The student who went off on me in class.

She comforted me and said she would try to get me back sooner. I was thinking *what?!* She came back to check on me. When I returned to school, the student came during office hours. She sat down and apologized for her outbursts. She explained her stressors and how she had a rough third shift.

I listened attentively and empathetically, and I was thinking, *I am glad I did not escalate the situation and I am glad my fruits of the spirit kicked in,*

Galatians 5:22

"But the fruit of the spirit is love, joy, peace, longsuffering, gentleness, goodness, faith, meekness, temperance, against there is no law."

Another profound emotional event that led to anxiety, stress, and bewilderment was when I was pulled from my class and asked to just sit in that class while a junior faculty was instructed to teach the class.

Let me put this in perspective. The students complained that I was teaching above their level and using words they did not know, therefore, they felt intimidated. The words used were from anatomy, physiology, and pathophysiology. My colleague presented the material which was very simplistic and for each response, the student received a hand clap and a statement of "very good."

I thought, *okay, I can always learn. You know, you're never too old to learn in terms of instructional strategies and different things.* I was okay with it. But at some level I felt that yet again, all eyes were on me.

The intention was to humiliate me, which I guess at some level it did. I thought, *why am I sitting here? I can't interact with the students, and I can't contribute to the instruction as part of the team.* It felt like I was being put in my place. But what place? I am doctorally prepared, with a Ph.D. and I am a NLN certified nurse educator with over 25 years of experience.

Dean X came in to speak with the students to smooth over their concerns. She didn't realize I was in the room. She went on to dismiss my teaching and informed them I would not be their teacher, nor would I be interacting with them. Her eyes glanced over the room and landed directly on my eyes. Her demeanor changed as I smiled.

After the class was over, she wanted to know why I was in the classroom. I informed her that the recommendation was for me to sit in as a guest and watch the instructor so I can learn something.

After those two events and trips to the emergency room, I was admitted for a full cardiac workup. I was diagnosed with angina—spasms of the coronary arteries—brought on by emotional stress. When I heard the diagnosis, I took a deep sigh and made an intentional decision about my health. I turned to faith and exercise. I had to learn how to provide self-care. I cared for students and patients, but also needed to pencil in renewal time for myself. I needed to schedule class time for myself and find someone to talk to about my experiences who wouldn't call me an angry Black woman.

I encourage you, if you're experiencing any physical symptoms, to seek medical care as soon as possible.

Chapter 15

Psychological Effects of Racial Bullying

When I looked at the psychological consequences, I was anxious. *Who's going to report? Who's going to say... what can I say?* So, the doctor put me on a low dose of lorazepam, reluctantly, but I told her, "You know, I can't sleep at night, I'm on edge." When you get to a point where you see the person walking in the hall and your chest tightens, that's a problem. That's extreme stress. I experienced different levels of anxiety.

I didn't want to take Xanax or Lorazepam my whole life, and they wanted to put me on other stuff. I don't think so. *I'm not depressed. I am NOT depressed.*

Let me share my experience on a psychological effect that resulted in hair loss. I had a full head of hair when I started this higher education journey to attain tenure. I take hypertensive medication. One of the side effects of that medication is hair loss. In addition, I have a genetic predisposition to alopecia. There were also hormonal changes caused by menopause that could have contributed to hair loss.

When asked about my baldness, I would reply by telling

people how it's a little bit about hormones, a little bit of side effects of medication, and a whole lot of stress because I was not able to share my feelings or verbalize my feelings. When I did, I would always be accused of being defensive.

"Why are you defensive or the angry Black woman?" So, I thought, *okay, nursing has taught me to be assertive. If I can't advocate for myself, how can I teach students how to advocate for themselves?* Hair loss did not contribute to my psychological wellbeing, body image, or self-esteem.

I had to get used to having my hair fall out and seeing spots of baldness in my hair. At some point, I had to decide. *What do I do?* Finally, I made the decision to just go bald, which was a psychological journey. Often, people thought I had breast cancer or some form of cancer. I was able to get out of that valley of despair and get refocused and know who I am. I am not my hair. Health is very important, and I had to get a handle on my health, not through medication or anything like that.

These are some of the health consequences and psychological events that I experienced from being exposed to racism daily. I had to deal with my peers telling me I looked intimidating, and I looked better wearing a wig. I asked an administrative assistant if she perceived me as intimidating. Her response was no, but she added she could tell why others would think that. She went on to say it takes a strong and confident woman to wear that look.

Because of the responses to my hair loss, I experienced psychological symptoms of anxiety and anger. At that point, I was thinking if it was worth it, being a nurse.

The Intersection of Racism on Mental Health and Feeling Invisible

Below is a combination of narratives that influenced the nurses' mental health.

There's nobody that looks like you. I have generally been the first Black in the unit. The White nurses usually don't have as much education or experience, and they can't stand that your credentials are higher than theirs, and you come in with these good ideas, but they are dismissed. You see them repurposed as another nurse's own ideas.

Another nurse mentioned, all they have to do is spread the lie about you and your progression up the career ladder is hindered because of lies being spread.

I was given difficult assignments while the White nurses were given light assignments. For example, I arrived at work and went into the report room. The charge nurse was sitting at the head of the table. As she read off the patient assignments, my case load had high acuity patients. These are patients who need more assistance, and the nurse or ancillary help will need more time to care for them. I glanced down at my assignment to find that I had all the patients who were obese. I looked up and asked her why she assigned me all the high acuity patients. When I heard her response, my mouth dropped to the floor. Her voice said, "Because you are obese, and I thought you would be more empathetic towards them." Wow, no crap. I have struggled with weight all my life. To hear the charge nurse—my colleague—call out my obesity was disheartening. I wanted to crawl under the table, I wanted to punch her, I wanted to get up and leave. The assignment was not changed, and I went on to care for my patients with empathy, dignity,

N THE INVISIBLE BLACK NURSE

and the respect that they would not receive from my colleagues.

The participant went on to say that she had to take a deep breath and recalled the scripture that says,

"I can do all things through Christ who strengthens me" (Philippians 4:13).

The participants were asked to respond to the following question:

Describe a situation where you felt not valued in your professional achieved role.

This participant took a deep sigh. This session was videotaped, and you could see the pain was still palpable. She recalled a time when she went up for promotion that required a master's degree. She went through the interview process and responded to each question appropriately. During the interview process, she was told that she was too much like the interviewer. She wondered why that comment was made as that should have nothing to do with her qualifications.

A week went by, and she was called to the Human Resources (HR) office and was informed that she did not receive the promotion. There was no indication that she was not qualified academically or skillfully. The participant worked for the organization for ten years. The HR person told the participant that she was too abrupt and too much like the person who interviewed her, and they figured it would be a clash. Again, this is an example of being blocked for promotional opportunities based on the perceptions of others. She was too blunt, too assertive. Really?

The next question posed was to describe a situation where you felt invisible.

The hiring committee always passed me over for the position. A new graduate nurse was hired over me to take the charge nurse position. With over 20 years of experience, I was overlooked for someone with less than a year experience. If you recall, the position called for a masters-prepared nurse.

The last question posed was to describe a situation where you were held to a higher standard than your peers (scrutinization).

Keeping in mind that the participant was overlooked for the position of charge that required a master's degree, there was a conflict with the implementation of a grant around patient care. The participant was told that she should have helped the charge nurse and told them what should be done to implement the grant since she has a master's degree that has a research component.

The participant responded by reminding the committee member that she was not hired for the position due to her bossiness and she should not be held accountable for the lack of competence the new graduate had in the implementation of grants.

Another participant wanted to share with White and other non-Black minority nurses that Black nurses have a heart and have the knowledge to provide evidence-based quality and culturally competent care as they were trained.

We should not be judged by our skin tone, as we had no choice on selecting the degree of melanin in our DNA. We should be given an opportunity to demonstrate our academic and God-given talents.

After a day's work, I go home, cry, and get in bed to do it all over again.

What would you (the reader) offer to Black nurses who may experience horizontal abuse, scrutinization, and delegitimization of the professional role? Take a minute and write down your thoughts:

_____

_____

_____

_____

_____

_____

A Compilation of Narratives

What It Feels Like to Be Invisible

It feels like watching George Floyd being murdered in plain sight. It is said in the legal world if you stand by and observe a crime, do nothing, you are just as guilty as the person committing the crime. As I watched via the television, I saw a man beg for a breath as the knee went more forcefully into his neck. As he yelled out for his mama, my heart started tightening up as I thought about my son who struggles with substance abuse and bipolar disorder. This could have been him. The arrogance of hands on his waist, as if nothing were happening. There was no humanity and no one rendering of aid. If that were a dog, there would be rendering of aid.

Similarly, when Black nurses encounter acts of incivility which can escalate to racial bullying, we ask for help, go up the chain of command, and meet the same resistance. We are not heard.

I saw this firsthand when I interviewed the nurses who participated. There is a shift in their expressions when recounting what they experienced. These are stories that happened years ago, yet it's like they're experiencing it again for the first time. Let's peek.

We have lived with educated people who are racists... People look at us and the first thing they see is this Black male. They see this Black female... When someone looks at me, they don't look at me as Dr. X, Director of the Nursing Program.

A physician actually called me the N word. I don't care what you say. It made me feel less important. I was given the most difficult assignments while the White nurses were given light assignments. I felt harassed and discriminated against. I was told by my nurse manager that I would be under a microscope and that they would be watching everything I did. This was not told to my White colleagues. The nurse manager did not intervene, and nothing was said to the physician.
There are times where it appears that my credentials are always questioned. I had a coworker give the wrong answer to a patient, but my credentials are always questioned. It makes me feel like I will always have to prove myself. I am at the table and not going anywhere.

Intellectual Hanging

Several nurses equated their experiences as the new form of "hanging." Instead of hanging you from a rope, they try and discredit your credentials, and this is considered intellectual hanging.

As I stepped onto the campus of California State University, San Bernardino (CSUSB), a sense of pride and anticipation filled my heart. Landing a position at a minority-serving institution was not only a career milestone but also an opportunity for eventual loan forgiveness. The prospect of having my $65,000 student loan evaporate after seven years of service was a beacon of financial relief.

With hope in my heart, I marched into the Human Resources office, eager to initiate the loan forgiveness process. The agent in charge, a gatekeeper to my financial freedom, met my enthusiasm with a cold, indifferent gaze. "The deadline is Wednesday," he stated matter-of-factly.

Undeterred, I calmly replied, "I know, and today is Monday. I'm here for you to sign the document, confirming my seven years of service to this minority-serving institution."

The agent, seemingly unmoved, insisted that the time frame was too short, refusing to extend his assistance. I left his office, clutching the unsigned document, bewildered and wondering how something that held such promise for my colleagues could be slipping away from me.

My coworkers reveled in the joy of impending loan forgiveness, a collective celebration that seemed to exclude me. The weight of my unfulfilled expectations bore down on me as I contemplated the ballooning debt—$65,000 had morphed into an overwhelming $225,000 at the time of this reflection.

In the midst of this financial quagmire, a prayer escaped my lips, pleading for divine intervention. "Lord, help me be visible in this moment of need. Bless the agent who refused to sign off on my seven years of service."

As the deadline loomed, I grappled with the reality that my path to financial relief had been obstructed. The invisible barrier, erected by the very person meant to facilitate the process, left me feeling stranded amidst the jubilation of my colleagues.

In the face of adversity, I clung to hope, trusting that visibility would eventually find its way to me. As I navigated the complexities of loan forgiveness, I held onto the belief that somehow, in some way, my plea for relief would be answered, and the invisible shackles of debt would be broken.

BECOMING VISIBLE

The following section describes Black nurses' thoughts on what they want to say to their peers in their own words.

Effective communication strategies are offered to start the conversation. Resilience factors are discussed and how to create a psychosocial healthy work environment.

BECOMING VISIBLE

Hey Barbie with the straight hair, why do you hate me so much? If you got a gripe with me, bring it to me and not the patients under my care. You got this?

I am puzzled… if you hate me, why are you laying under a tanning booth to look like me? Why are you inflating your lips to look like me? Why are you sitting in the sun to look like me? Why are you getting butt implants to look like me? Why do you hate me so much?

Because you hate you.

How to Communicate with Nurses of Color

Ephesians 4:29

Do not let any unwholesome talk come out of your mouths, but only what is helpful for building others up according to their needs, that it may benefit those who listen.

BECOMING VISIBLE

Proverbs 12:18

The words of the reckless pierce like swords, but the tongue of the wise brings healing.

First, one must respect diversity.

Second, acknowledge one's bias.

Third, one must listen with an open heart.

Fourth, one must actively listen with intention and purpose.

Chapter 16

Cross-Cultural and Racial Communication

What is effective? What is not?

The question I asked the participating Black nurses was: If they could have a conversation with their White colleagues, what would they want them to know? The responses ranged from solemn to forceful. "This is what I want you to know, Barbie, with the straight hair."

ᐅ When you dismiss my feedback, your foot is on my neck.

ᐅ When you try to embarrass me in front of others you discredit yourself and project your insecurities.

ᐅ I have value.

ᐅ I am empathetic and compassionate when responding to your verbal assaults.

ᐅ I looked through the eyes of diversity and through open-mindedness, it doesn't become such a black and white picture.

> Think about who you're going to take care of and how you are going to work with those that identify as Black or African Americans.

> We passed the nursing program, and we passed the national state boards (National Council Licensure Examination or "NCLEX"). There is no special test for us, no accommodation for being Black.

> Get to know who we are, invite us to functions, don't judge us based on others' perception of us.

> I have a right to seek opportunities for advancement without being hindered from you.

> Your behavior and actions force me to reflect on my faith and forgive you (Matthew 6:14-15: For if you forgive other people when they sin against you, your heavenly Father will also forgive you.)

> Take time to understand what it's like to walk a day in my shoes, not by getting tanned and modifying your lips and buttocks to look like me but walk a day in my shoes as a Black nurse.

> I feel invisible because you minimize my accomplishments, are dismissive of any recommendations that facilitate change, and show acts of superiority when communicating with me.

Wow. That is powerful. As you read this, what are you thinking? What are you feeling? How would you respond to your Black colleagues as they shared this with you?

Take some time to reflect. Below, you will find some space for you to write your responses.

In addition, the participants were asked about what behaviors characterized perceptions of racism. It was important to ask this question to gain an understanding of what interactions were perceived as racist. In addition, participants were asked to identify characteristics of racism they encounter in their work environment. Bullet points are used to immerse you into behaviors that you may not be aware of how Black nurses view them. Let's look.

Characteristics of racism emerged as the following:

- Feedback being ignored during meetings.

- Communication by White nurses come across as condescending.

- Being interrupted when speaking with other Black nurses or Black ancillary staff.

- Not being addressed by degree accomplishment.

- Not included in the decision-making process. My input is not acknowledged and yet I hear the same comments paraphrased by my White peer and she gets the credit.

- Nonverbal behavior that reflected indifference: a sigh, looking away, avoiding eye contact.

- Interactions that reflected condescending behavior. For example, I offered feedback regarding the misuse of concept mapping in place of a care plan. I verbalized that there are two approaches to concept maps— structured and unstructured. The original intent was to use in the clinical setting to evaluate the students' level of understanding using a visual tool of conceptual linkages. My peers dismissed my feedback by staring at me and then going on to talk about replacing care plans with concept maps. They went on to say that care plans were not used in real-life nursing. The real reason was they did not want to grade the care plans as it took too much time, and the adjunct faculty was not getting paid for the time it took to grade the care plans. I went on to explain that the care plan in education was an academic tool to transition the student from lay thinking to critical thinking in a linear format as this set the foundation to adapt to changes in the patient's condition. Again, my feedback was dismissed. My peers did not ask any questions or explanations for further understanding. I shook my head reflecting on my first dissertation topic was the use of concepts maps for ESL learners when reading textbooks.

- Accomplishments not being acknowledged verbally or in written announcements. For example, when speaking at a conference or when an award is given, it was not acknowledged via email or in the announcements of accomplishments.

- Being viewed as Black before being viewed as a nurse.

Take a moment to reflect on those characteristics and write down any thoughts or feelings you have toward these experiences. Have you been on the receiving end? Have you been on the doer's end?

Are you ready to use this information and reflect on how you communicate with those who look different than you? Who speaks differently than you? Who has a different worldview than you?

Chapter 17

Resiliency and Persistence

James 1:2-4

*Consider it pure joy, my brothers, when you are
involved in various trials, because you know that*

the testing of your faith produces endurance.

Galatians 6:9

*And let us not be weary in well doing: for in due
season we shall reap, if we faint not.*

How do these nurses survive the constant bombardment
of racial bullying from their colleagues and other
members of the heath care team? These nurses were
found to be resilient in their resolve to persist despite their
encounters of racist interactions. Let's look at ways they
demonstrated resilience and persistence.

Romans 5: 3-4

*... and not only that, but we also glory in tribulations,
knowing that tribulations produce perseverance,
character, and character hope.*

How do Black nurses cope and navigate the verbal assaults and questioning of their right to be acknowledged as a professional registered nurse? Most of the participants spoke about drawing on their faith to get through. There were some who spoke about ignoring the situation while in the workplace, but finding a safe space to discuss their experiences and talking to a trusted person who will listen and not interrupt their reality, Such as, clergy or other nurses with similar experiences. Some prayed amidst the storm.

One participant said:

*The prayer warriors would come to my office and
pray for me. They would acknowledge what I am
experiencing and know what I am going through in
my environment.*

*Some students would see me in the snack room, speak
to me and say, we know what you are experiencing.
We see it. You are a role model of perseverance and
we do not think it is right.*

Some were more assertive and confronted the situation, speaking truth to power only to be told they are aggressive, defensive, and angry. Wow, the angry Black woman syndrome. A few nurses spoke about engaging in non-healthy coping measures such as having a drink or two after work, wanting to lash out at the person through cussing or punching them out.

*I wanted to punch them right in their lying mouth so
they can see what an angry Black nurse feel like. I
will then ask for forgiveness from God.*

There is a fine line between sanity and insanity and these
nurses walked a fine line, some said a tight rope, to make
sure they stayed on the side of sanity. Their focus was on
providing quality patients and culturally competent care
regardless of what they were experiencing from their peers.
Those who were introspective spoke about experiences
where they needed to be resilient, but in the process, physical
and psychological health was affected.

Racial bullying was described as an imbalance of power.
It happens repeatedly. It's on purpose. There's a strong
emotional reaction, basic power exchange and control. They
have no remorse. They blame the victim and they do not try to
solve any problems. This led to personal stress. Participants
indicated increased stress, increased physical complaints,
increased psychological complaints in their professional
role. They indicated an increase in role stress, role strain,
and role conflict. They felt invisible, but they were still able
to care for their patients.

Chapter 18

Stories of Coping/Resilience

Coping Strategies

Participants were asked what type of strategies was used to cope with racism? Some used suppression of their feelings. Some use humor as a response to mitigate their stress. A few indicated the use of having a drink after work.

Let me share my experiences with you. How do I cope? I initially used suppression to cope with the behavior of my peers. I ignored the behavior and did not engage in verbal battle. When I'm at work, I do not engage in such nonsense because I am focused on providing safe, quality, and culturally competent care. The downside is that it led to internal stress that resulted in palpitations and baldness. Not addressing it with my peers landed me in the ER and being admitted far too many times. The last time I went to the ER, I made an intentional decision to stop internalizing and bring it out of the darkness into the light.

The use of humor is healing. I find myself laughing and smiling a lot. Anyway, being quiet did not work. When I spoke up for myself using professional terms, I was put into the category of the angry Black woman or being defensive. Why are Black women in the workplace, regardless of being at the start of their career trajectory or those at the top, are called angry Black women?

I make sure I listen before I speak. I honor the person. I respect that person as part of humanity. I also know that maybe they didn't intend it how it sounded.

You also must do a lot of self-reflection on your responses. Don't respond with a knee jerk response. Make sure you use your telephone voice, without inflection or rising because we will be accused of being aggressive and threatening.

I'll pull out a whole lot of scriptures and post them in strategic places in my office. I pause and look at those scriptures before I would speak, to help ensure that when I interact with someone, I'm saying things to edify them and not bring them down or add fuel to the flickering flame

Colossians 4:6:

"Let your speech always be with grace, seasoned with salt that you may know how you ought to answer each other."

Another verse used is

Proverbs 23:9

Do not speak in the hearing of a fool, for he will despise the wisdom of your words.

The recurring theme of resilience is grounded in faith-based strategies for the nurses that I've talked to and then confronting the matter respectfully with the person.

I secured a personal trainer and engaged in rigorous exercise twice a week just to get my stamina built up so I can endure the assaults that I will encounter in a healthier way.

To erase negative thoughts that came into my mind, I decided to use a technology example, and immediately hit the delete button and not even let the thoughts get to my ears to go through for processing. That technique has been good in terms of resiliency.

I also do not let my self-talk put me in a negative space. Remember that God made each of us unique. There is only one of you. Even if you're a twin you're different. As a twin you have different attributes. I understand that everyone may not believe in a higher power but knowing that God created each of us unique with our personalities and freewill, I respect you as part of humanity. I respect you as part of God's creation and that helps me persevere and be resilient.

I hope that through my respectful and uplifting responses to you that you would have a different approach moving forward when interacting with nurses of color.

Chapter 19

Creating a Psychosocial Healthy Work Environment

Do You See Me Now?

Creating a Psychosocial Healthy Work Environment

A group of nurses was asked what they would recommend to create a healthy work environment to eradicate racial bullying.

They had the following responses:

- Workshops on racial inclusion.

- Curriculum changes that include racism as a variable under cultural diversity.

- Seminars on communication patterns of racism.

- Historical and contemporary perspective of racism.

- Disseminate literature on racism in the form of incivility and racial bullying.

- Minority perspective on behaviors that reflect racism.

- How to mentor minority nurses.

- The health consequences of perpetual racism between peers, colleagues, and patients.

- Rules of engagement when interacting with Black nurses.

Creating a Visible Work Environment

How do we start the process of becoming visible? Do I wear a sign that says, "I am your Black nurse, willing to take care of you in spite of your indifference and hostility toward me"?

The question "Does your ability to provide quality and cultural competent care suffer because of acts of racial incivility you experience?" Most nurses indicated that there were no adverse effects toward patients. "We are tolerant of such behavior as we took an oath to provide care regardless."

I solemnly pledge myself before God and in the presence of this assembly, to pass my life in purity and to practice my profession faithfully. I will abstain from whatever is deleterious and mischievous, and will not take or knowingly administer any harmful drug. I will do all in my power to maintain and elevate the standard of my profession and will hold in confidence all personal matters committed to my keeping, and all family affairs coming to my knowledge in the practice of my calling. With loyalty will I endeavor to aid the physician in his work, and devote myself to the welfare of those committed to my care.

This pledge has been updated to be more inclusive of the times and references to purity and God were removed.

Ephesians 4:29

Do not let any unwholesome talk come out of your mouths, but only what is helpful for building others up according to their needs, that it may benefit those who listen

Proverbs 15:1

A gentle answer turns away wrath, but a harsh word stirs up anger.

These women were asked: "What are the rules of engagement? How would you like your peers to interact with you first?" Here are some of their responses.

They need to listen and not cut me off. When I first started talking about my feelings, they would tell me it can't be happening, we're in the 21st century. That response minimizes my feelings and does not respect my experiences. The response does not demonstrate respect or facilitate a conversation based on trust and honesty. Let me confront my reality. Let me share my reality with you. Let's clarify expectations of the communication process and create transparency. Let's engage in reflection of how our communication affected each other.

Reflect on your ability to be empathetic, to Blacks and other nurses who are different than you and who may hold contrasting opinions different in terms of race, ethnicity, culture, gender, sexual orientation, and gender identity(ascribed role) These stories will help give you a familiar foundation on how to be empathetic and how to respond to Black nurses who may be experiencing the phenomenon of nurses eating their young.

SUMMARY

I learned that you can't change another person's perception of you. You can't change their hostile acts toward you. You can't change the approach of this abuse. What you can do is change yourself. You may say, no way.

Reader's self-reflection:

Write down what behavior you have encountered and your response to that behavior. What would you do differently?

Locate and meditate on scriptures and words of affirmation that would keep you grounded.

_____

_____

_____

_____

_____

Chapter 20

Leveraging
Your Visibility

When you think about leveraging your invisibility, envision yourself at a stop sign. You are at a complete standstill. You look both ways before you go out into the street. When you encounter a challenge, stop before you speak, reflect on the consequences of speaking from a place of hurt. What could happen? Write down the positive and negative consequences on your physical health, mental health, and relationships at work.

_____

_____

_____

_____

_____

Now that you have weighed out the consequences, you can proceed to the yellow light, and proceed with caution. Proceeding with caution means to stop and pause before you speak. Reflect on how your words will impact others.

Remember, you do not want to add to the problem with your words.

Take a minute to use the sandwich method. This method is used by instructors when giving feedback to students. We say something positive about their work, give goal-directed and constructive feedback, and end with something positive.

_____

_____

_____

_____

_____

Now that you have mastered the red and yellow lights, you can proceed to the green light.

State how the experience makes you feel physically, behaviorally, and emotionally. You can phrase it as follows:

> ▷ Your communication with me made me feel…

> ▷ Your interaction with me made me think that…

Keys to Unlock Your Expertise

This chapter describes 10 keys to unlock your expertise. The term "key" in this chapter represents a key that provides a solution to a problem. A key that regulates and brings harmony and conformity. Therefore, leveraging your keys is integral with leveraging your expertise to become visible.

You can only control one thing and that one thing is you. You can't dictate how another may feel or what they may say. You can insert the key into the lock and manipulate how you turn it to bring harmony and to unlock your expertise. Just like you put a regular key in the door, if it's a micro millimeter off, it's not going to unlock the door.

> ▷ **Key One** to authentic engagement – Using assertive communication that promotes positive communication with others. Share your feelings honestly about the situation you are referring to. Use therapeutic techniques to frame your response and be aware of your nonverbal facial expression. Acknowledge that you are not attacking the person but responding to the behavior. For example, I had to discuss an issue with my dean that involved race. I drew on the strategies recommended by Stephen M.R. Covey (2018) that includes developing a trust talk, extending trust talk, and restoring trust talk. The recurring theme in all positive communication is to start with listening. Start with yourself to examine your intent. It is important to separate the person from the behavior in question. Make a behavior-specific request of the change you want to see and ask what you can do to facilitate resolution.

I entered the office where HR was in attendance via Zoom.

The dean had instructed me not to discuss the disease process of Sickle Cell Anemia and any other health disparities that involved African Americans. You can imagine, I was in total shock. I immersed myself in Covey's strategies as well as Lisa Nichols strategies on care confrontation with the intent to keep the relationship intact.

Here is the dialogue that was delivered: *Thank you for taking the time to discuss this issue that I need further clarification on. First, I want you to know that I do not think you are a racist. But the actions demonstrated I perceived as racist when I am being reprimanded for speaking about sickle cell anemia when it was part of the learning outcome on blood disorders (declaring my intent to make things right). I acknowledge my initial behavior was intense as I could not believe you would say anything like that when our mission and values include diversity and inclusion. I apologize if my demeanor were perceived as aggressive rather than assertive especially when you added that my vacation was revoked knowing that I was presenting at a conference, and I could not withdraw at this late date. My reality was that those behaviors were racist and intended to hinder me from achieving my professional development goals and discredit me with the organization in which I was scheduled to speak.*

In addition, our interaction caused me to have a high level of anxiety which resulted in an emergency room visit. Lastly, you have denied saying this or writing this in an email, which was later removed from the system. I am here to clarify what African American health issues can be discussed.

The meeting went well. We were able to maintain a positive relationship, my intent was clear, and I was able to separate out the behavior from the person. I can't say it was easy. She still had to think about reinstating my vacation which caused continued stress. I call these strategies "rules of engagement" when being authentic, courageous, and fearless.

As you read this scenario, how did it make you feel? What thoughts were evoked? Please take a minute and use the lines below to write them down:

_____

_____

_____

_____

_____

> **Key Two.** You must be prepared and competent to participate in the rules of engagement. Whatever strategies you decide to use, you must stay focused and stick to those strategies to maintain communication, one's esteem, and the relationship. You need to speak from facts versus an emotional response.

> **Key Three.** Empowering others using positive terms. For example, Galatians 5:22-23 says "But the fruit of the spirit is love, joy, peace, longsuffering, gentleness, goodness, and faith. Meekness, temperance, against such there is no law."   For those who do not subscribe to a faith, terms can be used that do not evoke feelings of being belittled, marginalized, anger, and words that impact self-esteem. That would start a positive space for communicating. Always remember you do not know what the other person may be experiencing that causes them to communicate in a less than professional way.

> **Key Four.** We need to maintain a positive attitude that projects integrity. You're a professional. You're representing your organization in the community or on the floor with your hospital affiliates, always assuring your positive attitude.

> **Key Five.** Remember to use active listening when engaging in communication with others. Your facial demeanor should reflect you are listening to understand the intent of the communication. Have you ever been in a conversation with peers, colleagues, or leadership and tuned out? By tuning out, did you miss out on some key communication that was needed to bring a positive outcome?

I want you to take some time and reflect on how you will eliminate distractions by actively listening. Write your response on the lines below:

_____

_____

_____

_____

_____

> **Key Six.** Have a teachable spirit. In non-faith terms, which translates into having a willingness to learn from others that may be younger or less experienced than you. For example, you've been in your position for a long time. We can always learn from the younger nurses incorporating new technology and different experiences. As nurses, we are lifelong learners. Be open to change with the current evidence and trends of our practice.

Students, if you're reading this book, have a willingness to learn from others who have traveled the road and been in the trenches. When seasoned nurses share information with you, their goal is to help you become the best version of yourself as an efficient nurse, a safe practitioner, and culturally competent nurse in order to manage a diverse workforce. Administrators, have a teachable spirit with a willingness to hear your employee's concerns and their perceptions of what's going on in the work environment and how that makes them feel physically, as well as psychologically to achieve conflict resolution while maintaining integrity of the relationship.

- **Key Seven** is forgiveness. Forgiving those who harm you. Forgiving those who sabotage you. Forgiving those who go to bed at night thinking about how they are going to stop you tomorrow or how they are going to hinder your progress financially, professionally, and personally. That's a hard one, but it can be done. You may wonder, how does this key unlock your expertise? You become a better version of yourself. You release anger and mistrust. You can execute your role responsibilities. Forgiveness will allow you to shine in your various roles

- **Key Eight** is praying for others. How do you pray for those patients who call you the "N" word and say they don't want the Black nurse to take care of them. How do you pray for your colleagues who tell lies about you or try and sabotage the care of your patients or students if in academia? Let me share with you an experience I had when I had to dig deep to learn how to pray and forgive those who maliciously tried to hurt me. I share this heartfelt story to help others who may encounter such an experience so they may know that you can grow from it. It still saddens me as I lay the words to these pages.

I have just attended a conference hosted by T.D. Jakes. I left feeling empowered, confident, encouraged, and fearless. I felt ready for my upcoming meeting to see if I was recommended for tenure and promotion. I felt confident knowing that my student evaluations have been favorable over five years and there were no remediation activities and no indication that I was not on track to be successful. It was the day of the meeting and I felt relaxed and self-assured with no obvious level of anxiety about the process.

I walked up the steps slowly, feeling fearless. As I entered the boardroom, I could see everyone sitting around the table. To my surprise, my mentor was at the table because she was out on sick leave. I was thinking positively despite our differences and thought she was there to support me. As I approached the table to take my seat, I focused on the facial expressions and they were all expressionless no smiles, just solemn. I felt encouraged that I was going to get the news that I've been waiting for, that I've met all the requirements, and I will receive tenure and promotion. Keep in mind, at that time, I've never gotten a negative evaluation from students. As I sat down, I glanced to my right and saw on the top of the folder, "Do not recommend tenure, do not recommend promotion." I was devastated. I was in shock. I could feel my heart beating faster and faster. I took a deep breath and refocused on the members.

How could I be denied this opportunity? My evaluations said I've been fine. I've gotten no verbal reprimands. I've not received any remediation plans for me. How could this be? How did you come to this decision? I graciously thanked them for their time and left the meeting. I walked back over to my office in a daze. I recalled my mentor telling me that I would be a better fit in a university setting. I later found out that my mentor made the decision that she didn't want me there.

She felt because I was working on my Ph.D. that I would be better suited to a university. She got out of her sick bed to come and put that nail in that coffin. She was that influential.

I also found out from students that she came to my clinical site to evaluate me, which was out of sequence. She was asking the students to offer negative comments about me. After she left, the students brought it to my attention, and they didn't know why she would be asking those questions about me. They felt that she was setting me up for sabotage. I tried to ease their minds. I said, "Well, we don't know, and we can't go on speculation." They wanted to speak up for me. I said, "No, you still must proceed through this school. So no, I'll handle it."

You may wonder, how does this example help with the key of praying for others who harm me. This was my first experience with blatant racism that caused me to be non-retained (terminated) based on one's opinion of me. To unlock your expertise, one needs to always respond professionally and extract the lesson from the experience to help others navigate a similar experience. I prayed for all of them and declared, Lord forgive them for they know not what they do (Luke 23:34)

> **Key Nine** Demonstrate your transformative leadership skills. Transformative leadership defined by Northouse (2019) is the ability of a leader to

create a connection among their team members that raises the level of motivation and morality. A leader who is attentive to the needs of motives of those who are followers with the intention of helping them reach their full potential.

What type of leader are you? Do you have the ability to empower others to lead? Are you a micromanager? Are you able to bring out others' talents for the good of the organization? Encourage your team to be empowered to release the leader within. Transformative leadership will produce the next generation of leaders.

> **Key Ten.** It's important that you have that spirit of understanding and spirit of empathy. When you travel the road of leadership in nursing, you must leverage your expertise by understanding the stakeholders at each position. For example, you must understand the role responsibilities of the administrator. You must understand the role and responsibilities of the dean. You must understand the role responsibilities of the provost, the role responsibilities of the chancellor, and how they all interconnect to help the organization be successful. Everyone has roles, responsibilities, and outcomes they must achieve. To unlock your expertise, to have that understanding of interconnection to demonstrate empathy when asked to do something at a minute's notice.

I hope this last chapter of the book on unlocking your expertise has helped you move toward visibility in your workplace. Before you can be visible in your workplace, you must be visible within yourself.

Moving forward:
Where do we go from here?

Thank you for taking the time to read this book. You have been taken on a journey to experience what it is like for a Black Registered nurse navigating the complexities of race in their achieved role as a professional registered nurse. The focus was limited to the interactions between their peers and other members of the health care team. The reading of this content may have caused you to pause and ponder, what can you do as an individual to be a social change agent to help create psychosocial healthy work environment and eradicate nurse bullying.

We have had the discussion and you have been immersed in the experiences of Black registered nurses who feel invisible in their role. You have engaged in self-reflection in response to those narratives. It is hoped that you have been inspired, motivated, educated, and ready to join the army of nurses who are ready to combat and eliminate racism in nursing and create an environment of inclusion.

Now that you have weighed out the consequences, you can proceed to the yellow light, and proceed with caution. Proceeding with caution means to stop and pause before you speak. Reflect on how your words will impact others.

—Ora V. Robinson, Ph.D., RN, CNE

APPENDIX A

Definitions

Interestingly, recent nursing literature uses terminologies such as "feeling invisible", "horizontal violence", "horizontal abuse", "lateral violence", and "nurse bullying" to describe racial discrimination in the workplace compared to previous studies that used phraseologies such as bias and bigotry. Here is how recent research describe these terminologies:

- Feeling invisible is described as not being acknowledged in the professional role as a nurse.

- Horizontal violence is described as experiencing negative attitudes from their nurse peers.

- Lateral violence is described as peer-to-peer verbal abuse.

- Nurse bullying is described one who mentally belittles, constantly criticizes, finds faults, and scapegoats.

- Horizontal abuse is described as insubordination, negative attitudes, and verbal abuse from Whites and other oppressed minorities.

- Scrutinization is described as the double standard being held to a higher standard than their White nurse peers.

- De-legitimization of the professional role is described as lack of acknowledgement, exclusion, and lack of professional interaction.

- Relational aggression is described as using a relationship versus physical harm to inflict social harm (female bullying, incivility, mean girls).

Additionally, the American Nurses Association (ANA) describes bullying as "repeated acts of behavior with the intent to undermine, humiliate, and cause distress in the individual."

APPENDIX B

Keys to Move Past the Pain and Toward Forgiveness

- Acknowledge that you are in pain.
  - » Consult your primary physician.

- Acknowledge the hurt you feel.
  - » Complete this sentence: I feel hurt because…
  - » Here you must be honest with yourself. Identify any fears. For example, my hurts were:
  - » I felt hurt because I followed the rules.
  - » I felt hurt because I was a team player.
  - » I felt hurt because I was not valued as part of the profession.
  - » I felt hurt because my credentials were minimized or ignored.

- Understand that it is not about you.

- There is a history of isms in the United States of America and there is residual and re-emergence of behaviors that work to hinder another's movements to achieve higher levels of learning, ranks in nursing profession, and career choice.

- Know your history to put your experience into perspective. The good news is we are not being hanged or burned at the stake. That behavior has translated into intellectual hanging and burning at the stake through defamation of character.
  » Process the event with someone you trust.

- It is best to discuss with someone who has traveled that journey.

- Discuss with your spiritual advisor.

- Process with someone who can give you insight on progressive movement.
  » Enter your prayer closet.

- Reconnect with your spirituality.

- Attend support groups for minority nurses who are denied tenure and promotion.

- Pray for the following:
  » Understanding
  » Healing
  » A compassionate heart o
  » How to forgive.

- Read Martin Luther King's letter from Birmingham jail.

- Read Paul's letter from jail in the Bible.

- Speak out your frustrations to someone you trust, or out loud to yourself.

- Replace negative thoughts with positive thoughts.
  - » Be angry at the behavior and not the person Remember when you have a relationship with the Lord, the devil works through others to cause you to doubt.

- Forgive the person because they don't know what they are doing.

- Pray for the person/s to have prosperity and good health.
  - » Yes, you must do this. Remember it is not the person, it is the behavior.
  - » Offer a smile, do not engage in hostile behavior toward another.
  - » Tell the person/s you forgive them.

- This is very healing.
  - » Continue to support the person

APPENDIX C
Bibliography

Carnegie, M.E. (2000). *The Path We Tread: Blacks in Nursing Worldwide,* 1854-1994. *Third edition.* Jones and Bartlett Publishers, Inc., and National League for Nursing.

Ciocco, M. (2018). *Fast Facts on Combating Nurse Bullying, Incivility, and Workplace Violence.* Springer Publishing Company. New York, N.Y.

Covey, S.M.R. & Merrill, R.B. (2018) *The Speed of trust: The one thing that changes everything.* Free Press New York, NY.

Dellasega, C. (2011). *When Nurses Hurt Nurses: Recognizing and Overcoming the Cycle of Bullying.* Sigma Theta Tau International Honor Society.

Dellasega, C. (2019). *What to Do When Nurses Hurt Nurses: Understanding and Resolving Relational Aggression and Bullying in Nursing.* Sigma Theta Tau International Honor Society.

Dellasega, C. (2021). *Toxic Nursing: Managing Bullying, Bad Attitudes, and Total Turmoil.* Sigma Theta Tau International Honor Society.

Gupta, T.D. (2009). *Real Nurses and Others:* Racism in Nursing. Fernwood Publishing, Winnipeg.

Hardy, M.E. & Conway, M.E. (Eds.). *Role theory: Perspectives for health professionals.* Appleton-Century-Crofts, New York, NY.

Hassouneh, D., Akeroyd, J. Lut, K.F. & Beckett, A.K. (2012). Exclusion and Control: Patterns Aimed at Limiting the Influence of Faculty of Color. *Journal of Nursing Education, Vol. 51, No. 6.*

Hine, D.C. (1989). *Black Women in White: Racial Conflict and Cooperation in the Nursing Profession,* 1890-1950. Indiana University Press, Bloomington & Indianapolis.

King James Bible (n.d.). King James Bible Online. https://www.kingjamesbibleonline.org/ (Original work published 1769)

Nichols, L. (2020). Three tips for creating life-changing relationships, YouTube. (https://www.youtube.com/watch?v=Mdz6x9Iq9Aw)

Northouse, P.G. (2019). Leadership: Theory and Practice. Sage Publications, Inc. Thousand Oaks, Ca.

y Muhs, G.G., Niemann, Y.F., Gonzalez, C.G. & Harris, A.P. (2012). *Presumed Incompetent: The intersections of Race and Class for Women in Academia.* The University Press, Boulder, Colorado.

Robinson, O.V. (2013). Telling the Story of Role Conflict among Black nurses and Black nursing Students: A Literature review. *Journal of Nursing Education Vol. 52, No. 9.*

Robinson, O.V. (2014). Characteristics of Racism and the Health Consequences Experienced by Black Nursing Faculty. *The ABNF Journal.*

Abstract, Robinson, O. (2009). Nursing students perceived experiences with racism in nursing and its impact on cardiovascular changes, psychological well-being, and learning outcomes. *Advances in Qualitative Methods.*

Staats, C. (2015-2016). Understanding Implicit Bias: What Educators Should Know. *American Educator*

Stanley, C.A. (2006). *Faculty of Color: Teaching in Predominantly White Colleges and Universities.* Anker Publishing Company, Inc. Bolton, MA.

Threat, C.J. (015). *Nursing Civil rights: Gender, Race in the Army Nurse Corps.* The Board of Trustees. University of Illinois.

Williams, D.R. & Williams-Morris, R. (2000). Racism and mental health: The African American Experience. *Ethnicity & Health 5(3/4), 43-268.*

APPENDIX D

Permissions

The National League for Nursing (NLN) has given permission for the following material:

1. National League for Nursing. (2018). Percentage of Minorities in Basic RN Programs by Race-Ethnicity. Biennial Survey of Schools of Nursing, 2018. Retrieved from: http://www.nln.org/docs/default-source/defaultdocument-library/percentage-of-minorities-enrolledin-basic-rn-programs-by-race-ethnicity-2018-(pdf) cdadc95c78366c709642ff00005f0421.pdf?sfvrsn=0

2. National League for Nursing. (2019). Distribution of Student Instruction by Faculty Type and Nursing Program. Faculty Census Survey, 2019. Retrieved from: http://www.nln.org/docs/default-source/defaultdocument-library/distribution-of-student-instruction-byfaculty-type-and-nursing-program-2019-(pdf).pdf?sfvrsn=2

3. National League for Nursing. (2019). Distribution Full-Time Nurse Educators by Race, 2019. Retrieved from: http://www.nln.org/docs/default-source/defaultdocument-library/distribtion-of-full-time-nurseeducators-by-race-2019-(pdf).pdf?sfvrsn=2

THE INVISIBLE NURSE
With Dr. Ora Robinson

About the Author

Dr. Ora V. Robinson is a highly accomplished individual in the field of nursing, with a passion for education, wellness, and eradicating racial biases in the nursing profession. As a certified nurse educator through the National League of Nursing, she has demonstrated a commitment to excellence in nursing education.

Dr. Robinson has received the prestigious Young Publisher's Award through the Association of Black Nursing Faculty, showcasing her dedication to advancing the visibility and recognition of Black voices in nursing. Her National Board Certification as a Health & Wellness Coach (NBC-HWC) and Mayo Clinic certification as a Wellness Coach reflect her commitment to promoting holistic well-being in both her professional and personal life.

She holds a Graduate Certificate in Evidence-Based Coaching, emphasizing her expertise in using evidence-based practices to empower individuals in their wellness journeys. Dr. Robinson's research is centered on minority nurse role conflict, with a specific focus on Black Registered Nurses experiencing racism in the nursing profession. This work highlights her dedication to addressing and mitigating systemic issues within the healthcare field.

Beyond her academic and research pursuits, Dr. Robinson is a globetrotter, having traveled to four continents—Africa, South Korea, India, and Israel. This international exposure enriches her perspective and contributes to her holistic approach to nursing education and wellness coaching.

Dr. Robinson's personal mission is to inspire, motivate, and educate one nurse at a time. Her overarching goal is to eradicate racial bullying and other "isms" in the nursing profession. As the author of "The Invisible Black Nurse: Navigating RACE-isms," she provides a guide on becoming visible in a profession where underrepresentation is a significant challenge. Her book, infused with the principle that "Love covers all," serves as a beacon of guidance and empowerment.

A well-sought-out speaker on racism in nursing, Dr. Robinson actively engages with various professional organizations, sharing her insights and advocating for positive change. Through her multifaceted contributions to nursing education, wellness coaching, research, and advocacy, Dr. Ora V. Robinson exemplifies a leader dedicated to creating an inclusive and equitable future for the nursing profession.